Wakefield Press

The Death of Dr Duncan

Tim Reeves completed a Bachelor of Arts degree with first-class Honours at the University of Adelaide, with a thesis on the impact of Dr Duncan's death on gay law reform in South Australia. He has produced a wide range of academic work as well as journalism and poetry. His first book, *100 Canberra Houses: A Century of Capital Architecture* – co-authored with Alan Roberts – earned the Clem Cummings Medal from the ACT Institute of Architects. His second was *Winning Homes: 75 Australian House Design Competitions*. He is currently at work on *Adelaide Modernism: 101 Houses*.

Also by Tim Reeves

100 Canberra Houses:
A Century of Capital Architecture
(with Alan Roberts)

Winning Homes:
75 Australian House Design Competitions

THE DEATH OF
DR DUNCAN

Tim Reeves

Wakefield
Press

Wakefield Press
16 Rose Street
Mile End
South Australia 5031
www.wakefieldpress.com.au

First published 2022

Copyright © Tim Reeves, 2022

All rights reserved. This book is copyright. Apart from any fair dealing for the purposes of private study, research, criticism or review, as permitted under the Copyright Act, no part may be reproduced without written permission. Enquiries should be addressed to the publisher.

Best endeavours have been made to contact all owners of copyright material. The publisher will be pleased to correct any inaccuracies in the next printing of this book.

Cover designed by Stacey Zass
Edited by Julia Beaven, Wakefield Press
Typeset by Michael Deves, Wakefield Press

ISBN 978 1 74305 893 0

A catalogue record for this book is available from the National Library of Australia

Wakefield Press thanks Coriole Vineyards for continued support

This book is dedicated to four very special people who have supported me on my 30-year journey with the Duncan case:

Malcolm Cowan (1940–2020), Dr David Hilliard OAM,
Ian Purcell AM (1946–2016) and Will Sergeant

The following chapters in this book have been
published previously:

Chapter 8: Tim Reeves, 'The 1972 Debate on Male Homosexuality in South Australia', in Robert Aldrich and Garry Wotherspoon (eds), *Gay Perspectives II: More Essays in Australian Gay Culture* (Sydney: University of Sydney, 1994).

Chapter 9: Malcolm Cowan and Tim Reeves, 'The "Gay Rights" Movement and the Decriminalisation Debate in South Australia, 1973–1975', in Robert Aldrich and Garry Wotherspoon (eds), *Gay and Lesbian Perspectives IV: Studies in Australian Culture* (Sydney: University of Sydney, 1998).

CONTENTS

Preface		ix
Introduction		1
PART I	**SETTING THE SCENE**	
Chapter 1	Adelaide in 1972	9
Chapter 2	Dr Duncan the Man	15
Chapter 3	The Drowning	35
PART II	**THE DUNCAN CASE**	
Chapter 4	Police Investigation	63
Chapter 5	Coroner's Inquest	78
Chapter 6	New Scotland Yard Report	101
Chapter 7	Reopening of Case and Trial	121
PART III	**GAY LAW REFORM**	
Chapter 8	1972 Decriminalisation Bill	143
Chapter 9	1973 and 1975 Decriminalisation Bills	165
Conclusion		185
A Pictorial Record of the Duncan Case 1972–2022		189
Timeline		207
Glossary		211
Image Acknowledgements		223
Acknowledgements		224
Index		226

THE MELBURNIAN

University of Melbourne

DEGREE CONFERRED SEPTEMBER, 1947
Bachelor of Dental Science.—N. A. deC. Dwyer.

DEGREES CONFERRED DECEMBER, 1947
Bachelor of Laws.—A. N. L. Atkinson, R. L. Ellenberg, C. H. Francis, T. V. Ottaway.
Bachelor of Mechanical Engineering.—T. T. Ferrero, A. Jodell.
Bachelor of Science.—F. W. Farr, P. J. Knuckey, I. McDowell, S. A. Prentice.
Master of Dental Science.—W. A. Dott.
Master of Arts.—S. H. Heymanson.
Diploma of Diagnostic Radiology.—C. R. Laing.

MATRICULATION EXAMINATION, DECEMBER, 1947
Special Exhibition (Greek).—G. I. O. Duncan (aeq.).
General Exhibitions.—G. I. O. Duncan, B. N. Gill.

CLASS LISTS
First Classes
French.—G. I. O. Duncan, G. Sargood.
Latin.—G. I. O. Duncan.
Greek.—G. I. O. Duncan.

G. I. O. DUNCAN

B. N. GILL

G.I.O. Duncan and his examination results from the *Melburnian*

PREFACE

In May 1948, Melbourne Grammar – one of Victoria's and the country's most exclusive private boys' schools – published its regular magazine, the *Melburnian*. This included the results of university entrance examinations from the previous year, with photographs of the school's top two students.

On the right was B.N. Gill (it was then the norm to be identified by initials rather than given name) who had won a General Exhibition, which usually carried a money prize. Gill was a relaxed, if formal, figure in front of the camera.

On the left was the 17-year-old G.I.O. Duncan, who had easily eclipsed Gill in the scholastic stakes with a General Exhibition as well as a Special Exhibition in Greek. He had also won three First Classes in Greek, Latin and French.

Duncan's portrait was an essay in stiffness. His lips refused to reveal even the hint of a smile and his eyes looked vacantly into the distance.

In a little over two years Duncan would be removed from his home to a sanatorium for treatment of tuberculosis. Within four years he would be an orphan of independent means. Nine

The Death of Dr Duncan

years later he would enter Cambridge University and earn a PhD. In 1966, while teaching at the University of Bristol, colleagues would describe him as 'a mystery'.

On the morning of 11 May 1972 Dr Duncan's body was pulled from Adelaide's River Torrens where it had lain for 10 hours. Ten days later the press reported that three Vice Squad officers were being questioned over the death of Duncan, a newly appointed, 41-year-old law lecturer at the University of Adelaide. Soon after it was disclosed that he had been killed at a homosexual beat.

Within 11 weeks there would be the first attempt in South Australia and Australia to decriminalise male homosexual acts. In 1975 South Australia became the first jurisdiction nationally to embrace gay law reform.

This is the story of the unsolved murder of Dr George Ian Ogilvie Duncan, and how it ultimately transformed the state, nation and English-speaking world.

INTRODUCTION

In 1989 I enrolled at the University of Adelaide as a mature-aged student to do a Bachelor of Arts degree. By the time of my Honours year in 1992 I had decided to write a thesis on Dr Duncan, whose dreadful murder was now 20 years old and still unsolved. And so, 2022 is a double commemoration for me. It is a pearl anniversary – 30 years on and off researching and writing about Dr Duncan, the case and gay law reform. But it is also the 50th anniversary of his violent and senseless death.

My thesis led to an invitation in 1993 from the *Australian Dictionary of Biography* to write on Duncan for Volume 14. I had little idea that nearly 18 months of work and letters sent all over the world to seek or clarify information would produce a mere 600-word entry. Yet it encapsulated not only the tragedy of his story but also its complexity and richness.

There was an unexpected find with the discovery that the South Australian Coroner's Court held a suitcase belonging to Duncan, the only item then known to remain of him. As I had moved to Canberra for work, my colleague Malcolm Cowan stepped in to investigate.

The Death of Dr Duncan

He was led down a maze of stairs to a small room in the basement of the court where a battered leather suitcase with a broken handle sat on a table. There were boxes of pills from a murder trial and a baby crib with a bouncinette in it. It was, as he said, 'bizarre'. But he was left to his own devices and over several days catalogued the contents of the suitcase which contained what little there was of Duncan's personal papers. Remarkably, he also found a number of manilla envelopes, which contained many of the initial police interviews of people involved with the Duncan case. These documents were transcribed by Malcolm who, sadly, died in 2020.

In 2015, when I was co-curating an exhibition commemorating 40 years of gay law reform in South Australia, a formal request was made for the suitcase to be included. I was advised by the then manager of the Coroner's Court that it had been destroyed. When Simon Royal of the ABC took a closer look at the issue, he discovered that the decision had been made by the Major Crime Investigation Branch of SA Police. The outgoing coroner severely criticised this act, which had been done without consultation. He said he would not have agreed to it.

That suitcase was a piece of the state's cultural heritage. It should have been kept or, even better, donated to an institution like the State Library of South Australia for preservation and display. It is a black mark against SA Police when they could

Introduction

have been generating goodwill. Especially when, even after all this time, the odour of possible police involvement in Duncan's death is still pungent.

Then Simon Royal discovered personal items belonging to Duncan: his watch, wallet, cufflinks and glasses. For decades they unaccountably had been held by State Records of South Australia where presumably they could have been freely accessed. But in 2016 they had been transferred to SA Police.

With work proceeding to develop *Watershed*, the oratorio about Duncan's death planned for the 2022 Adelaide Festival, a request was made to view and possibly photograph the items so they could be replicated for the production. This was denied by SA Police on the grounds the Duncan case was still open. How an object such as Duncan's glasses could be so crucial potentially to solving the case that they couldn't be seen by impartial observers was not explained.

My involvement with SA Police was not finished yet. Matters took a strange turn in 2021 when a plaque originating from Britain and bought at an auction in Adelaide was reported on by the redoubtable Simon Royal. It had been presented by SA Police in 1972 to the two detectives of New Scotland Yard who had been called in to reinvestigate the Duncan case after the coroner returned an open finding. It was a small plaque of timber with the SA Police logo sitting on top. Engraved into sterling silver were these words: 'Presented to the Murder

Squad New Scotland Yard by the South Australia Police. To mark a pleasant association, Adelaide, August–October 1972'. This apparently was standard practice when police forces from different countries collaborated on a case.

New Scotland Yard plaque

SA Police seemingly was unaware that this 'pleasant association' had produced a report which had concluded that the three Vice Squad officers linked to the case were guilty.

Introduction

The Crown Solicitor at the time, however, had decided there was insufficient evidence to proceed with a prosecution.

The report was released publicly 30 years later in 2002, ironically after two of the Vice Squad officers had been acquitted in 1988 of Duncan's manslaughter. I recall reading the report. When I reached paragraph 129, which described Duncan's death as 'merely a high-spirited frolic which went wrong', I froze for several minutes as the impact of those words set in. They are still as shocking to me today as the killing itself.

Tim Reeves
Adelaide, January 2022

PART I
SETTING THE SCENE

CHAPTER 1

Adelaide in 1972

In 1965 John Bray published an article on his home town of Adelaide. He was a bohemian – a poet and playwright – but also a lawyer and future Chief Justice of South Australia. Adelaide was, he began, 'a city of moderation' – which seemed neither particularly congratulatory nor condemnatory – though by the end of the piece he was veering toward the latter by describing its 'depressing rectitude'. But change was in the air. The state had just discarded 32 years of conservative rule and within five years would embrace three transfers of political power, with four premiers. By 1972, with a population nearing 900,000, Adelaide was on the cusp of radical social and cultural change. On 12 May, its inhabitants awoke to read the first of what would be many newspaper stories about the death of Dr Duncan.

For decades the monolithic figure of Premier Tom Playford, sustained by a hefty electoral gerrymander, had towered over South Australia. His Liberal and Country League Party had an almost single-minded focus on economic development, which had led to car production becoming the state's biggest industry, and a resultant severing of Commonwealth handouts.

But public spending on sectors like health and the arts had declined. The signature Adelaide Festival of Arts was only created in 1960 through the efforts of local civic leaders and captains of industry, many of whom belonged to the exclusive male-only Adelaide Club, which wielded enormous financial and social power. Playford believed that cultural activities should be mostly privately funded, and he 'was unperturbed by those who regarded South Australia as the wowser state'.

In May 1970, and for the second time, Don Dunstan was appointed Premier of South Australia – a position he would go on to hold for nearly a decade. He was determined to stamp his mark on a city and state which he believed had become stultified and small-minded. Adelaide indeed had gained a reputation for 'sobersided attitudes, restraint, even dullness', where hotels closed at 6 pm and drinking in restaurants after 8 pm was proscribed. These restrictions had been swept aside in a previous short-lived Labor administration, but Dunstan was now focused on expanding his vision for creating in the capital city an 'Athens of the South'. He would triple government funding to the 1972 Adelaide Festival, establish new arts institutions and construct major cultural facilities as part of his aim to make the state 'the artistic centre of Australia'. His succeeding governments would also relax censorship laws, abolish the death penalty, advocate for Aboriginal land rights and support the rights of women. Decriminalisation of

Adelaide in 1972

male homosexual acts would be achieved as well after three attempts by private member's bills from both sides of politics.

Dunstan's party may have controlled the Lower House of South Australia's Parliament (House of Assembly) but confronted the gerrymander most potently in the Upper House (Legislative Council). But by 1975, under a more democratic electoral system, and with the conservative opposition split between what was now the Liberal Party and Liberal Movement, Labor had increased its numbers. Gay law reform could never have been achieved that year without these developments.

Adelaide relied on the reporting of politics from its two main newspapers: the morning *Advertiser* and evening *News*. The *Advertiser*'s chairman, Sir Lloyd Dumas, had been unabashedly pro-Playford but the *News*, under the direction of the hands-on Rupert Murdoch, had been more critical of the administration. In the 1960s the *Advertiser* was regarded as sober to the point of insipid in comparison to the eastern states dailies: 'There lingers about it still the aura of the nineteenth century provincial organ'. But it had a circulation of roughly one-fifth of Adelaide's population and, its confident conservatism aside, was the preferred read of the middle classes. Dumas' retirement in 1967, however, ushered in a new era with editors more inclined to support progressive causes. The *Advertiser* would provide extensive coverage of the Duncan case and play a leading role in gay law reform.

This was also a time when the Church held substantial sway in the South Australian community, and religious leaders were often asked to comment on social issues or matters of morality. There was a wide range of denominations but also conservative Christian lobby groups such as the Community Standards Organisation and Moral Action Committee. In 1969, when the South Australian Parliament began the process of enacting abortion law reform, the views of its opponents were widely reported and a wealth of letters to the editor was published. Gay law reform would provoke a similarly vigorous response.

The tertiary sector was also widely respected by the populace, with academics held in high regard. Dr Duncan's employer, the University of Adelaide, first established in 1874, was the state's pre-eminent tertiary institution, and especially its Law School where he would work. In 1949, and in a rare move, Playford had doubled its annual grant and it had taken its place among the nation's principal universities. Its substantial site in the city lay between North Terrace and Victoria Drive, along the southern bank of the River Torrens. In the 1930s a footbridge had been constructed over the Torrens to connect to the university's sports ovals on the northern side.

Adelaide had been laid out so its site spanned the Torrens as the main river. The main bridge was City Bridge, which extended Adelaide's key thoroughfare – King William Street/

Adelaide in 1972

A long stretch of the Torrens beat as viewed from University of Adelaide footbridge (site of attack marked with asterisk)

Road – to North Adelaide. From City Bridge to the University of Adelaide footbridge, on the southern riverbank, there were walking tracks and flora, boatsheds for various rowing clubs, and public toilets for men and women. There was also a small police station to monitor activities on the river and in its vicinity.

In 1972 this area was a well-known 'beat' or meeting place for homosexual men. At a time when male homosexual acts in public and private were criminalised, beats were important places, providing both sexual and social contact with other homosexuals. For many they offered the only opportunity for encounters with like-minded men. Beats could be in public toilets, parks, lookout areas and the like, where quick, anonymous sex could be had on the spot. Alternatively, people could meet and depart by car for the privacy of someone's home. Some men made friends or met lovers or life partners in this way but, for others, beats were only ever for casual sex.

However, in the postwar years homosexual men came to be seen as a threat to the nation's moral health and security, on par with that of communism. In South Australia there was a dramatic increase in the policing of beats, including the use of decoys in entrapment. The South Australian Vice Squad was tasked with monitoring beats, and being charged could result in a trial, a prison term and social ignominy – even suicide. It was not only the peril of arrest, as increasingly police were assaulting men as well. That is, assaulting them as a deterrent, or for sport, or both, knowing victims would not report the attack. Over time the risk of encountering other bashers (mainly young men) also escalated.

The Torrens beat is the site where, on 10 May 1972, Dr Duncan was thrown in and drowned. So, who was this man?

CHAPTER 2

Dr Duncan the Man

George Ian Ogilvie Duncan was born an only child on 20 July 1930 in Golders Green, London. In keeping with a custom that had developed in England, one enforced by his mother, he was called by his second name. This is revealed in his private correspondence and confirmed by a cousin: 'His mother chose the name Ian and he was always known by this name, *never* by George.' The man who is understood almost universally as Dr George Duncan was, in fact, Dr Ian Duncan. He was correctly identified by one newspaper early in the case, but all reporting that followed referred to the apocryphal George. This confusion is unsurprising given Ian had been in Adelaide for just seven weeks before his death.

Both Ian's parents were born in New Zealand. He would inherit his third Christian name from his father, Ronald Ogilvie Duncan, who was well-advanced in years, being 53 at Ian's birth. A chartered accountant by training, he was a successful businessman. He had been a dashing man in his early days in Christchurch: a prominent sportsman – a predilection not inherited by his son – and racehorse owner.

Ronald and his first wife Mabel, who later died, were married in Sydney to save embarrassment to their families as he was a Presbyterian and she was a Catholic. Ronald's second wife, and Ian's mother, was Hazel Kerr Duncan (née Martell). She was 19 years younger than her husband but, at that time, older than were most women when they married. Hazel had grown up in Dunedin. After her marriage, as was expected in the 1930s, she became a full-time housewife.

Ronald's daughter from his first marriage – Ian's half-sister – was known as Billie but had been baptised Mary Magdalene, which may have been bestowed on her by a devout mother. Ian's mother, Hazel, was an Anglican. Three different religious traditions in Ian's extended family may have led him in a new direction, one that satisfied his spiritual and emotional needs. As a young man he embraced Anglo-Catholicism – that movement within the Anglican Church that emphasises its Catholic inheritance and identity. Ian spoke freely and devotedly about his religious faith. His head of department at the University of Adelaide recalled: 'Dr Duncan had told me repeatedly that he was dedicated to the high Anglican tradition.' Duncan's funeral service was a Requiem Mass at Adelaide's best-known Anglo-Catholic church, St George's, Goodwood.

One relative remembers Ian as 'a little fair haired curly boy' when the family was farewelled departing England for New

Zealand in 1933. There is little other information, except for his education, that expands our knowledge of his early life. When his suitcase was discovered and his personal papers examined, the only photograph was of his freshman class at Cambridge. There was not a single image of his parents or early family life. Given what we will come to learn about his upbringing, it is quite possible he had destroyed any such records. His was not the happiest of childhoods.

The Duncan family came to Victoria in 1937 when Ian was seven, as Ronald was opening an Australian branch of his export firm. Ian attended Melbourne Grammar's Junior School as a day student, completing his education in the Senior School. It is not known if high academic standards were set by Ian himself, or his parents, or both, but his results were exceptional. He won numerous prizes and scholarships during his time there, including the Rusden Scripture Prize, Rosa Lascelles Prize for English Essay, Alexander Leeper Memorial in both Latin and Greek, and John Hugh Sutton Scholarship. He was named head of the school (essentially, dux) in his final year.

A close analysis of the records, however, reveals that his achievements were scholastic only. He did not excel in other activities like sport or debating, or take a leadership role. The posts of prefect/probationary prefect and house captain/ vice captain, for example, eluded him. A picture emerges of the classic solitary swot: his head so buried in his books that he engaged little with other students or the broader school community. No fellow students came forward to the media with stories about him after he died.

In 1940 Hazel started to display symptoms that were diagnosed as the early stages of cervical cancer. She died four years later, aged 49, as Ian was entering Year 9 at school. How this impacted him is unknown. Billie had married and moved away, so Ian was raised by his father, now in his mid-60s. As to this relationship we can rely on information from a Phyllis Hindmarsh who cared for both Ronald and Ian when they became ill with tuberculosis. She said that she nursed Ronald first and, later, Ian. Given the highly infectious nature of the disease it is likely to have been transmitted from father to son. This cannot have been easy for Ian as he had matriculated with brilliant results and entered the University of Melbourne in 1948 to do a Bachelor of Arts degree with Honours in Classical Philology (the study of ancient languages in historical sources). At the end of second term of his third year, the attack of tuberculosis forced him to withdraw from the course.

Phyllis Hindmarsh wrote to a colleague of Duncan's. She was genuine and respected because Ronald left her £50 in his will (she is referred to as 'Sister Hindmarsh'), and one-tenth of his estate if Ian predeceased him. She said:

> Ian had a most unfortunate upbringing (Dickens would not have imagined worse). If he was not quite normal in his behaviour – it was not his fault but that of background.

What can one infer from such an extraordinary statement? Aside from comically repulsive characters, Dickens conjures up poverty, social deprivation and Victorian-era rigidity. A boy educated at one of Melbourne's elite private schools would not meet the first criterion. But the second and third could easily play out through emotional abuse. It is difficult to judge but there is a hint in information disclosed by another third party.

A Harold Glover wrote to Duncan's head of department revealing that he and Ian had met as patients in the early 1950s at the Gresswell Tuberculosis Sanatorium near Melbourne. Through a shared interest in architecture Harold came to know Ian 'reasonably well':

> I was told by a Sister at the sanatorium that the circumstances of his admittance were unusual: that a very possessive father had wished Ian to stay at home for treatment of his T.B. but that as it was a fairly serious case, the then Superintendent ... went to the Duncan home and would not leave until Ian's bag was packed and he came with him to Gresswell in his car.

Harold added that Ian was visited by only one person. He was unsure whether she was an aunt or housekeeper (most likely it was Phyllis Hindmarsh) and her visits were infrequent.

The Death of Dr Duncan

Harold said that Ian, as far as he knew, had only his father, that he understood Ronald was unwell himself and he never visited. Clearly, there were no schoolmates or other friends in the picture. It is unknown for what period Ian may have been stranded at the hospital before and after Ronald died at the family home in Caulfield in January 1952. Ronald suffered from heart disease, but his death certificate also recorded pulmonary tuberculosis as a co-morbidity. He was 75.

Ronald's death notice from the newspaper is telling. It contained only the barest of information. Ian and Billie were not mentioned and there was no reference to a loving relationship with their father. Bizarrely, he was even misnamed as Robert. There also were no details of the funeral – indeed, no notice was ever placed. Ronald left the bulk of his estate to Ian because Billie had been provided for under the terms of her grandfather's will. Within two days of probate being granted the family home was advertised for sale. Ian clearly felt no attachment to it; possibly it held memories he wished to erase. As noted, there were no family photos found in his suitcase. It is difficult not to conclude that Ian suffered from a fraught, likely controlling, relationship with his father whose sporting prowess, ease of sociability and other talents he was unable to match.

At 21 Ian was now an orphan, but also a wealthy one. His father's estate included the family home and another property plus a share portfolio. It was all valued at over £13,500, more than $500,000 in today's money, but Ian could only access it from the age of 25. He drew up his own will with Billie as sole beneficiary. It would be one of the many ironies of the Duncan case that Billie died in November 1970 but Ian, a law academic, did not update his will. Either he had not maintained contact with his half-sister or simply overlooked the matter. He thus died intestate in 1972 and his estate was divided between a group of cousins.

In January 1956, six months after coming into his inheritance, Ian departed for Britain. The following year he received the news that he had been cleared of tuberculosis. One of the myths that sprang up in the early days of the case was that the illness had necessitated the removal of a lung. This belief has gained sufficient currency to be accepted as fact, appearing in numerous books, newspaper articles and websites. It is a fallacy. In his job application to the University of Adelaide, Ian acknowledged that the disease had been prolonged but declared that 'my health is now fully recovered'. And the autopsy report referred to the lungs (plural), and noted that no existing medical condition had contributed to or hastened death.

It is not known what drew Ian to Britain but it is known that he went with the names of the mother and sister of his friend from the sanatorium, Harold Glover. Ian made contact and immediately established a close bond with them. There is reliable information about these relationships because of letters found in Ian's suitcase. Dorothy Glover was single and older than Duncan (she playfully called him 'Unky'), an accomplished pianist and organist who lived with her mother whom she referred to as 'Mummie G'. She and Ian shared a deep religious faith. Harold reported that Ian 'seemed to want to spend as much of his holidays as he could touring with my mother and sister'.

Dorothy Glover at the organ in St John's Anglican Church, Launceston, Tasmania

In 1957 it was Dorothy who, according to Harold, gave Ian 'the necessary shove about going to Cambridge and eventually drove him there in her car'. Ian matriculated in the Faculty of Law and entered St John's College in September. He elected not to seek affiliated status based on his outstanding University of Melbourne results, essentially re-starting his tertiary education from scratch. He graduated with a Bachelor of Arts degree in 1960, and the following year with his law degree and, surprisingly, not with a First but Class IIA Honours. One of his tutors remarked that in large measure this was due to 'inherent nervousness' (he was not well-disposed to examinations) and his age (he was 31). Nevertheless, he commenced his PhD examining the High Court of Delegates, which heard appeals from ecclesiastical courts and the Admiralty from the time of Henry VIII. He completed his higher degree quickly – within three years – by 1964.

By this time Dorothy was living in Tasmania; she returned to Britain in 1966. In May of that year she wrote three letters to Ian. It is clear that her feelings for him have deepened over time and, after revealing them, she has been firmly rebuffed. She wrote: 'I just had a premeditation that something would go wrong, it was another way of convincing me that I had correctly identified you, even as long ago as 1956' (when they met). One does not have to read between the lines to know that she is referring to Ian's sexuality. In imploring words in one letter she wrote:

The Death of Dr Duncan

Dearest Unky

Do you remember many years ago in Dorchester when we found it necessary to apologise to each other, we managed to forgive immediately?

I hope it will be possible again now. In spite of the fact that I pray most earnestly every day for guidance in everything I do, and every situation that presents itself, I find that by doing whatever seems right at the time, I am capable of being very hurtful ...

This morning mother asked me if I had heard from Ian and I said, 'I am afraid I have done the wrong thing entirely and I have hurt his feelings. I shouldn't have said what I said, such things should only be said at the right time and that certainly wasn't it' ...

I only wish we could go back to that Tuesday, when the sun shone, the atmosphere was perfect, and the fields were full of bluebells, God was in His heaven and all was well with the world. Kyrie Eleison.

Love from Me.

Ian drafted a letter in response to her entreaties; it is not known whether it was sent as it was undated. It was heartbreakingly cruel, and here perhaps one can appreciate better Phyllis Hindmarsh's reference to an upbringing worse than Dickens:

There is a hint in your very obscure letter that you now realise that marriage is out of the question and you blandly imagine that we can both go back to the position we occupied before you began your extraordinary misconduct ... The feelings which I always had for both your mother and yourself were exactly the same. I looked upon you as one looks upon an aunt and now that that relationship has been destroyed, there can be no going back.

Your letter also implies that you feel that all you have done is to 'hurt my feelings' as you put it. You must be very unperceptive if you imagine that that is all that your wanton behaviour has done. Disgust and revulsion are words by no means too strong to describe my reaction to your improprieties and but for my firm conviction that you are not in your right mind I should express myself in language much more emphatic.

Do, please, understand that you are ill (perhaps seriously ill) and that you should be in the hands of a doctor.

It is not known what repulsed Ian more: the fact that Dorothy knew he was homosexual (and from the moment she met him) or that, armed with this information, she still loved and even wanted to marry him. It is also possible his disgust was fed by a sense of self-loathing.

Soon after, and perhaps with a desire to escape Dorothy, Ian gained employment at the University of Bristol. He taught part-time there from 1966 to 1971, the one academic post he held between completing his doctorate and moving to Adelaide. It was not a success. Ian's existence as an only child, the parental controls imposed on him, his studiousness which seemed to exclude everything else, his disconnection with other children and school life generally, had manifested into awkwardness and taciturnity as an adult. Any description of him invariably involved the use of words such as 'quiet', 'reserved' and 'retiring', potentially problematic traits in a workplace where communication skills are essential. One Bristol law academic, who believed Ian was asked to leave or that his contract was not renewed, commented:

> Duncan was an intensely shy man who found it very difficult to communicate with colleagues. I was very surprised when he was appointed because he seemed to lack the basic personality qualities desirable for teaching ... There seemed to be a complete lack of rapport between him and the students that he taught. His time at Bristol was short and rather unhappy for him ...

However, Ian had another side which challenges a further myth that has arisen – that he was essentially a loner. In his suitcase were recent letters from three couples who spoke of previous visits and invited him to stay again, including one who said they were looking forward to seeing him at Christmas. The husband subsequently described his longstanding and close friendship with Ian. As well, a Mrs Richards wrote to the Registrar of the University of Adelaide:

Dr Duncan the Man

In this little Essex village, we were shocked beyond measure, when we read of the tragic death of Dr George, Ian, Duncan. It was here that he had spent all his vacations, even in his Cambridge days and he had a large circle of friends.

We also know that in 1960, when Harold Glover and his wife visited England, the four Glovers and Ian went on holiday to Germany. Ian also attended at least one dinner with university colleagues in Adelaide and was described as a convivial guest. It is obvious then that he was not solitary and was able to relate meaningfully to others in social situations. He was comfortable with men and women, and with singles and couples, and his death had a profound impact on those who expressed it in writing. There is no evidence, however, that he enjoyed friendships with other homosexual men or relationships that involved intimacy.

On finishing work at Bristol, Ian started looking for full-time employment. He sent unsolicited applications for teaching positions in universities like Cardiff, Edinburgh, Exeter, Leicester and Oxford in Britain (one presumes he also approached Cambridge), and the Australian National University, La Trobe, Melbourne and Monash in Australia. In August 1971 he enquired about a possible vacancy at the University of Adelaide, and was advised that applications were open. A typed letter with his awkward signature and accompanying curriculum vitae arrived soon after. He was a Cambridge graduate whose PhD had recently been published in book form, and by Cambridge University Press; on paper he was impressive. He was capable, he said, 'of teaching most subjects commonly offered by a Law Faculty'. As well, the university was seeking someone to lecture in Roman law and legal history; both were Ian's specialties. Two references were sought, the University of Bristol's notably not alluding to his poor communication skills.

The recruitment process was overseen by the head of the Department of Law, Professor Horst Lücke. An assessment committee concluded that Ian 'was clearly the best qualified of all candidates'. By November he was being offered a lectureship in law, at the entry level but on the top salary scale of $9286 per annum, conditional on a medical certificate which would confirm his recovery from tuberculosis. Ian cabled the Registrar on 14 December accepting the position. Everything was in train until the arrival of a telegram: 'REGRET UNABLE ACCEPT LAW POST: DUNCAN'. Ian advised in a letter following that something had 'turned up' in England and he wished to avoid the upheaval of moving. And then, two weeks later, that arrangement had fallen through and he was writing again to ask whether he could be reconsidered for the job – to which the university quickly acceded. The initiation of gay law reform in South Australia obviously would have followed a

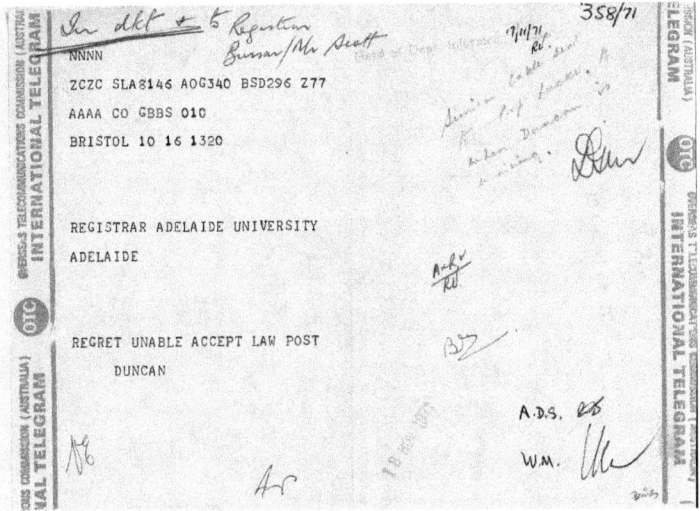

Ian Duncan's telegram rejecting his job offer

very different path had Ian stuck to his original decision, let alone that aged 91 he may still be alive.

Ian stepped off the SS *Orcades* on 25 March 1972, having travelled first class at the university's expense. He had been away from Australia for 16 years. He had ticked the 'Indefinite' box of his passenger arrival card which asked about his intended length of stay. Lücke met him and noted that he seemed 'terribly frail and he wasn't able to carry luggage well'. But he had departed England during winter and spent five weeks at sea, and may simply have been unsteady coming down the gangplank. Ian was conveyed to Lincoln College in North Adelaide – a Methodist residential college – where he

The Death of Dr Duncan

Ian Duncan's passenger arrival card

had rented a two-bedroom flat. He had only two days to settle in before commencing work on the 27th. He was pleased that the enrolment in Roman Law was 35; he noted that in Bristol he had never had more than eight. He had informed Lücke that the 9 am start time 'will help curb one of my most inveterate vices (remaining in bed too late in the morning)'.

Ian had brought with him his membership card for The Gaytime Friendship Society, which in 1969 was touting itself as 'Britain's largest gay male organisation'. He also had recent editions of the international gay travel guide, *Spartacus*. This identified meeting places in Adelaide like the Toledo Room of the Ambassador's Hotel in the city, and the Caribou Bar of the Buckingham Arms Hotel in Walkerville. But the guide also listed 'Outside Cruising' spaces which included Victoria Drive. Lincoln College was only a short walk to his new workplace, taking him over the University of Adelaide footbridge. If Ian had chosen to walk to work the footbridge provided the opportunity – looking to the right – to take in the sweep of a swathe of riverbank leading up to Victoria Drive. This was known as the 'No. 1 Beat'. It operated between City Bridge and the footbridge, and sometimes further afield, and had functioned since before 1910.

There is no evidence Ian had used beats (or 'tea rooms' or 'cottages' as they were known in Britain) in Cambridge or Bristol, but it is not an unreasonable assumption given how

The Death of Dr Duncan

AUSTRALIA continued

LAUNCESTON, Tasmania
BRISBANE BAR, Launceston Hotel

Outside cruising:
City Park (AYOR)
Princess Square (AYOR)

ADELAIDE, South Australia
TOLEDO ROOM, in Ambassador's Hotel, King William Street (Downstairs)
★ CARIBOU BAR, In Buckingham Arms, Walkerville Road, Walkerville
ISADORA'S LATE NIGHT SUPPER CLUB, (B4)

Outside Cruising
Elder Park, Victoria Drive
Victoria Park, Racecourse
West Beach
Glenelg Beach area
Broadway

Facilities:
1st Floor of David Jones Store and 5th Floor (AYOR)

ELIZABETH, South Australia

Facilities:
Town centre
The North
The Park
Grove Shopping Centre

WHYALLA, South Australia
THE SPENCER HOTEL BAR

Spartacus reference to Adelaide's homosexual attractions

quickly he acquainted himself with Adelaide's homosexual attractions. He had to be careful, however. It was ironic that he had arrived from Britain where male homosexual acts had substantively been decriminalised in 1967, to a country where no state or territory had adopted such legislative change. He could not afford, especially as a law lecturer, to engage in any illegal activity which might see him before the courts. It would have been ruinous for his professional reputation. As well, he had not earned a decent income since inheriting his father's estate 15 years ago. His suitcase revealed that he had expanded Ronald's share holdings, but they were no guarantee of financial security.

For now, though, he had to concentrate on his teaching and developing relationships with his academic peers and superiors. It was not an auspicious start. Professor Lücke would report to the Vice-Chancellor:

> Although I had come to respect Dr Duncan as a colleague, his own formal manner and the respectful mode of address upon which he insisted ('Professor'), despite repeated suggestions on my part to abandon it, prevented anything in the nature of a personal relationship from arising.

Dr Duncan, recently appointed at the age of 41 in his first full-time position as a base-level lecturer, was expecting his head of department and a professor in his own right to address him with the same title. And he persisted even when challenged. This could be an example either of academic snobbery or insecurity. Was it evidence of the rarefied existence in which Ian seemingly had lived most of his life, or simply representative of his sense of entitlement as the Cambridge scholar? Or was it a man who was out of his depth and, ill-equipped socially and professionally to cope, was now making absurd demands?

There was trouble brewing. The book on which Ian's doctoral dissertation had been based – *The High Court of Delegates* – had been well-received to this point and probably had cemented his job offer. But it would soon be reviewed by a Flinders University academic, Peter Howell, also Cambridge-educated but in history, and a fastidious scholar. His assessment of the book would find it seriously wanting. The review would ultimately appear in the *Historical Journal*, an imprint of Ian's own publisher.

But Ian Duncan would never live to read it.

CHAPTER 3

The Drowning

On Friday 12 May 1972 the *Advertiser* reported a story on page 9 under the heading: 'Car keys clue to body in river'. It revealed that police had recovered the body of a man from the River Torrens the previous morning, and were searching nearby streets to match the keys with a car, which may have been driven by him into the city on the Wednesday night. Police were treating the man's death as murder. They were seeking four or five young men who had allegedly thrown the dead man and a second man into the river from the southern bank between City Bridge and the University of Adelaide footbridge, close to Kintore Avenue. The second man was identified as Roger Wesley James, who had been admitted to the Royal Adelaide Hospital with a broken ankle. The dead man was estimated to be aged between 30 and 40, 185 centimetres tall with a slim build, of fair complexion with brown hair turning grey, and had blue eyes.

The body had been located by the Underwater Recovery Squad of SA Police about 12 feet (3.7 m) from the bank and in about 10 feet (3 m) of water. It was lying face upwards on the

WHERE THE DO

Advertiser story with an aerial photo of the No. 1 Beat (drowning site marked as 2)

Television, Page 23

21, 1972.   Phone 51 0421. Classified only 51 0261

CTOR DIED

DUNCAN INQUEST

I saw vice squad man at river' CONSTABLE TELLS CORONER

A vice squad policeman told a uniformed policeman to go away the night Dr. George Ian Ogilvy Duncan drowned in the River Torrens.

riverbed. Once retrieved it was placed on the riverbank with the lower legs dangling over the edge. A wrist bore a Smiths Everest watch which had stopped at 11.07 pm. A watchmaker later testified at the inquest that the watch was not waterproof, and so this was noted as the approximate time the body had entered the water.

Television footage of the retrieval of the body had been taken by a cameraman named Bob Perry. It was broadcast by Channel 7 and became folklore in Adelaide newsrooms. The body can be seen dressed formally, with a shirt and tie, but rigor mortis had set in and the arms were gruesomely outstretched. Later in the footage the body was transferred to an ambulance for transportation to the morgue, with the arms erect under the white sheet. Perry arrived on the scene having missed the body being retrieved from the river; it was returned to the waters and pulled out again for filming. The general feeling among police apparently was that it was a drunk who had accidentally fallen in. A drunk or not, the treatment by police of a corpse in this way is an appalling act of desecration.*

To assist with identification the body was searched for dry cleaning or laundry tags, and for markings like tattoos, but none were found. Police believed the dead man was English

---

* The recovery of Duncan's body has been spliced into a 1972 *This Day Tonight* story which can be seen at: https://www.abc.net.au/archives/80days/stories/2012/01/19/3411558.htm.

because a spectacles case containing glasses was found in his hip pocket with the stamp of a Cambridge optician; he also had a vaccination mark. There was nothing else to identify him, apart from his car keys. These opened a white Vauxhall Viva bearing a parking ticket and found at the third parking bay on King William Road, a short distance from the No. 1 Beat, but not directly on Victoria Drive. The car was traced to a George I. Duncan of 45 Brougham Place, North Adelaide, the address for Lincoln College. Dr Duncan's body was formally identified on the Saturday by his colleague, Professor Alex Castles. It was first-term holidays at the University of Adelaide.

The parking of his car and the lack of anything on his body that could generally identify him suggested that Duncan had been extremely cautious before entering the beat. Police would later discover his wallet on the top of a wardrobe in his flat.

Duncan's body was transferred to the West Terrace Mortuary soon after its recovery. Death was formally certified at 10.45 am by the pathologist, Dr Colin Manock, who then carried out the post-mortem examination. Duncan was recorded as being dressed in dark-grey trousers, a blue-and-white shirt, maroon tie, dark-grey socks and black shoes. Manock noted that there were 'diffuse horizontal abrasions' on the back of the body, and grip marks on each upper arm. He commenced his internal examination of the body, removing the major organs and conducting histological examinations of the tissues. The lungs, he noted, 'showed grossly distended alveoli with numerous ruptures of alveolar cells' – signature signs of drowning. Water removed from the Torrens contained diatoms (microscopic algae) in five different species, which were found in approximately the same proportion as the lung tissue.

Manock completed the examination and prepared his report. He concluded:

> The cause of death was fresh water drowning consistent with the River Torrens close to the point from which the body was recovered. The bruises on the upper arms of the deceased in the form of grip marks suggest that at least two people held him firmly shortly before his death. The abrasions on the back of the body are consistent with injuries sustained during a fall on to a relatively soft surface but are suggestive of a horizontal angulation or edge of this surface ...
>
> There was no natural disease present which could have contributed to or accelerated this death by drowning.

A controversial finding of Manock's would be revealed at the inquest. He finished the autopsy the day after the death – on 11 May.

The following day Roger James, his leg in plaster, was taken back to the river to reconstruct events. James' evidence was crucial for, aside from the attackers, he appeared to be the only witness to the events that led to Duncan's death. At the inquest he stated that he had been sitting on a bench on the lower path

The Drowning

7.   724/72.

CONCLUSIONS.

The cause of death was fresh water drowning consistent with the River Torrens close to the point from which the body was recovered. The bruises on the upper arms of the deceased in the form of grip marks suggest that at least two people held him firmly shortly before his death. The abrasions on the back of the body are consistent with injuries sustained during a fall on to a relatively soft surface but are suggestive of a horizontal angulation or edge of this surface.

No attempt was made to estimate the time of death as I was informed that the time of the deceased's entry into the water was relatively well fixed, and after the passage of some 8/10 hours' immersion any estimate would necessarily cover a wide interval of possible times.

There was no natural disease present which could have contributed to or accelerated this death by drowning.

The post mortem examination did not reveal any injury which would suggest that the deceased was unconscious when he entered the water.

C. H. Manock.
C.H. MANOCK, M.B., Ch.B., F.R.C.P.A.
Director of Forensic Pathology.

The conclusions of Dr Manock's autopsy report

by the River Torrens before standing up to watch a duck in the river. He was then approached by a man from his right who asked, 'Do you take it or give it?' before repeating the question, to which James replied, 'Neither.' While this conversation was taking place James became aware of a group of men who were coming down from the upper path to his left. At the point they reached him one of them – Duncan – was pushed into the river, his buttocks hitting the bank before he slid in. The man addressing James then joined with the others to attack and also throw him in. He broke his ankle on wooden pilings at the water's edge as he entered the river. He cried out that the other man was drowning, but was pushed back in after he tried to clamber out. He could see only the arms reaching upward and top of the head of Duncan, who had made no sound as he went in and was drowning silently. One of the attackers now stripped to his underwear and plunged into the river in an unsuccessful attempt to locate Duncan. The men then fled the scene. James crawled in agony up to Victoria Drive and hailed a passing motorist who took him to hospital.

The driver said at the inquest that James was in such a state of shock that he refused to be assisted into the car, was saturated and covered with leaves, and crying. The car was driven by Bevan Spencer von Einem who, in an astonishing twist, was convicted in 1984 of the murder of teenager Richard Kelvin. His name has also been mentioned in relation to the unsolved killings of four young men in Adelaide between 1979 and 1982.

Roger James moved to Sydney nine days after the drowning, which he claimed was pre-planned and coincidental. He returned for the inquest. Most of what is known in relation to

The Drowning

Site of attack on Duncan and James

how Duncan died is based on his evidence at the inquest. Over the decades, however, new information has come to light – including from James himself – which reveals inconsistencies and contradictions in his version of events. A key issue relates to why James was on the riverbank that night.

James stated at the outset that he was not doing the beat. When initially interviewed by two police inspectors they reported: 'He denied that he was a homosexual and that he was at this particular part of the Torrens for any ulterior purpose.' At the inquest he said he was there 'just to enjoy the peace'.

The Death of Dr Duncan

```
THE CORONER CALLS:    ROGER WESLEY JAMES,
                      18 Rainford Street,
                      SURRY HILLS, N.S.W.

                      Unemployed (SWN)
```

MATHESON   Q. How old are you?

A. 27.

Q. On Wednesday, 10th May, 1972, you spent the evening at various places in Hindley Street, Adelaide?

A. Yes.

Q. At some stage, you left that area to walk to your home?

A. Correct. I was then living at 2 Prospect Road, Fitzroy. I didn't own a car.

Q. Had you spent the evening in company with a friend in Hindley Street?

A. Yes. I left her about twenty to eleven.

Q. Did you proceed to walk home along King William Street, Adelaide?

A. King William Road, in a northerly direction.

Q. When you got to a position near the City Bridge, what did you do?

A. I crossed over King William Road and walked across the lawn to Victoria Drive.

Q. Do I understand by that you had been walking on the western side of King William Road.

A. Yes. I crossed over Victoria Drive and was walking up Victoria Drive in an easterly direction.

Q. Where did you intend to go?

A. I intended walking along the banks of the river up over the University Bridge to go home the back way there to North Adelaide.

Q. At some stage did you decide to sit on the seat near the river?

A. Yes.

Q. Why?

.../2

James' evidence at the inquest

The Drowning

This was confirmed in a 2005 ABC television story when the reporter stated: 'In describing that night Roger James debunks many myths, starting with the assumption that he was doing the Torrens beat. He says he was merely walking home when he was attacked.'

In relation to the man who propositioned him just before the attack, James admitted to police that 'I knew what he wanted' and on television he claimed that it was 'not the normal approach on a beat or anything like that'. This suggests that he was familiar with beat behaviour. In an August 1972 story that appeared in the Australian Union of Students' newspaper, *National U*, a person identified only as 'Mr P' said:

> I know James quite well and I know how he operates. I'd seen James in town the day before [the death] and had a big talk with him and asked him about how he was going with the bogs [beats], the drugs and all that shit. He didn't mention anything about leaving for Sydney.

In an article in the *Advertiser* James described this and other newspaper stories as containing statements about him in relation to the Duncan case that were 'vicious lies', but the conversation with Mr P is alleged to have occurred the day before the drowning. The New Scotland Yard report also concluded that James was 'known among homosexuals as a frequenter of the Torrens Lake site', indicating that he was familiar with and a user of the No. 1 Beat.

At the inquest James explained how he came to be on the riverbank that night. He stated that after a late dinner in the city with a friend he declined her offer to drive him home. Instead, he walked down Hindley Street, then King William Road before crossing over to Victoria Drive. He said: 'I intended walking along the banks of the river up over the University Bridge to go home the back way there to North Adelaide.' James was then living at 2 Prospect Road, Fitzroy. The most direct route therefore was down King William Road and into O'Connell Street in North Adelaide, which links with Prospect Road. The route he took went via Victoria Drive, the footbridge, War Memorial Drive, Brougham Place and, if he continued generally northward, Lefevre Terrace connecting with Main North Road and Fitzroy Terrace. This is a considerable detour which could hardly be described as a 'back way'. He also claimed he had taken this route 'two to three times' and 'in the evenings' in the prior 14 months he had been living in Adelaide. So he had done this several times, always including the riverbank and always at night.

In 1980 James was interviewed for a story in the Flinders University student newspaper *Empire Times* to coincide with the eighth anniversary of the drowning. The story stated that James 'wandered down by the River Torrens, toward an area notorious in gay circles for being a well-established homosexual pick-up place – a "beat"'. It quoted James as admitting: 'I suppose I was probably going to do the beat.' James also acknowledged at a 1986 preliminary hearing that although at that time he had been in a relationship with the cabaret singer Tony Monopoli, theirs was an open one.

The available evidence thus points to James as being a user of beats, and familiar with the No. 1 Beat. It also includes an acknowledgement that he was there on the night of Duncan's drowning to cruise the beat. At the preliminary hearing James admitted to lying under oath at the inquest, and also later to the New Scotland Yard detectives, but the subject of the lie was suppressed by the magistrate. It is not known therefore if it relates to this issue or another one.

Male homosexual acts at the time in South Australia – in public or private – were criminalised. Being on a well-known beat was not in and of itself a criminal act – the Torrens riverbank after all was for the use of all South Australians. Nevertheless, James' concealment that he was homosexual and doing the beat that night raises questions about the reliability of other evidence he gave, to the police and subsequently. This includes whether James was there that night without any preconceived plans or for an assignation – and specifically with Dr Duncan.

James has maintained that he had never met Duncan before the night of the drowning, and that he did not interact with him in any way on the night. The police record of interview with James at the hospital soon after the event has James saying: 'I've never seen the man before and do not know his identity.' But the following morning in another interview James was reported as saying that it was *Duncan* who had first propositioned him. However, the physical descriptions of the two men were different. James corrected this statement when he met with detectives the same evening and emphasised it in a new statement to SA Police. He confirmed it in a later interview with the *Advertiser*.

At the inquest James reported that on being pushed back into the river by the attackers one of them said: 'Save your mate.' The term 'mate' implies that Duncan and James did know each other, but James was not questioned further. Were they together that night, or had they been seen on another night by one or more of the attackers? As well, staff at the Royal Adelaide Hospital – and there were two of them – claimed that James had said: 'My mate has been drowned in the Torrens.' James responded at the inquest that he did not use the word 'mate'. When asked whether he used the sentence with the word 'friend' he said only: 'Not to my knowledge.' He did not unequivocally reject uttering the statement. Then during the 1988 trial James was asked whether he had said at the hospital: 'Get the coppers, get the coppers, my mate has been thrown in.' James responded that he did not use the words 'copper' or 'mate', but again did not disavow using the sentence with similar wording.

The New Scotland Yard detectives were convinced that Duncan and James did know each other. They interviewed a couple who had entertained Duncan at dinner on 9 May – that is, the night before his death. According to them at 11 pm 'he abruptly left the company, giving them the impression that he had a further appointment elsewhere'. Of course, this does not mean Duncan was going to the No. 1 Beat, and specifically to meet James. The Yard report claimed that Duncan's trousers contained paint chippings, which were a match for the bench James was sitting on. Nevertheless, no one came forward with evidence that Duncan and James were sitting on the bench at the same time, nor that they were conversing with each other.

In an earlier *National U* story of June 1972, several witnesses reported they saw Duncan and James struggling with members of the Vice Squad by the roadway before they were dragged down to the river. This differs from James' account that the attack happened on the riverbank. These seem to be Witnesses B, C and D, who were then promised protection by Premier Dunstan, but if it were them they had changed their story by the time they gave evidence at the inquest. They reported seeing men fighting but made no reference to Duncan or James.

In June 1972 the press also disclosed there was a man who claimed to have directly witnessed the death, but was too scared to come forward, although the story was quickly discounted. This likely was the man who was interviewed by New Scotland Yard and who gave a statement to police the following year; he was revealed during the later trial to be Robert (Bobby) Callaghan. Callaghan, who died before he could give evidence, said he had been drinking with Duncan and James at the Buckingham Arms on the night in question, and was with them afterwards at the Torrens. Duncan would have known of this hotel from his copy of *Spartacus*. Callaghan said Duncan and James were great friends and he had later seen James 'shaking' Duncan – but good-humouredly – at the beat. Dr Manock admitted at the inquest that the bruises on Duncan's upper arm could have been produced by a 'very forcible grip for only a very short period'. Callaghan said he:

> heard yelling, saw four men going along a path and three men run over a wall to a lower path to where Duncan and James had been walking ... one had grabbed James's feet and two grabbed his shoulders, and threw him into the river ... Duncan had stood there and then was also thrown into the river.

Of course, if James had been thrown in before Duncan then this is the reverse of what we understand from James' own account.

This was staggering new information, which completely challenged what had been accepted for over 15 years. But the

The Drowning

New Scotland Yard report did not even allude to Callaghan, perhaps with the knowledge that one of the protected witnesses claimed to have been at the Buckingham Arms up to 10 pm but made no mention of sighting Duncan or James. It is not known if police investigated this in 1973 and, if so, what conclusions they formed, but if the case had been reopened no charges were laid. James said at the trial: 'I don't accept Callaghan's statement at all. It is either fabricated on the part of whoever has written it, or he is having trouble with fantasy.'

Given that James went out of his way to hide the fact he was doing the beat that night, was it because he also had to conceal that he planned to meet or coincidentally had met another man for what may have involved criminal activity? At the inquest James was unable to explain how he did not hear the man approaching him from the right as the path was gravel. The New Scotland Yard report concluded that Duncan and James were sitting together on the bench, and this was the reason Kevin Williamson – who was sitting on a bench on the upper path and thus would have been a possible witness to an assault – was aggressively warded off by the attackers. But as will be demonstrated in Chapter 5, this theory lacks credibility.

James has never changed his story: during the police investigation (and even correcting an initial instance of misreporting); at the inquest; to the New Scotland Yard inquiry; at the preliminary hearing and trial; and during the 2005 ABC television interview. As well, no one else came forward with information to confirm that Duncan and James were friends – which would have been a quick relationship to have developed within seven weeks – nor that either of them earlier had been seen drinking together. However, the New Scotland Yard detectives tried to locate four men aged around 30 (James was 27) who were seen dining individually with Duncan. Taken together with Callaghan's statement and the initial – but uncorroborated – claims of alleged witnesses, combined with multiple statements in relation to Duncan and James potentially being 'mates', this means that the possibility they had met before cannot be discounted. Neither can the possibility that they were together at the time of the attack, whether by chance or choice, although the likelihood is low.

James has also insisted that he was unable to identify the men who threw Duncan into the river. Of the man who propositioned James and then joined with the others to throw him in, and who later stripped down to his underwear and dived in to try and find Duncan, at the inquest James initially stated that he probably would but couldn't be certain of identifying him. When he was recalled and pressed on the matter, he said he thought it was Constable Cawley, but was not definitive. But James in any case had provided a very good description:

The Drowning

> He was wearing a light grey suit, had dark hair, which was short in the front, had long sideboards. I think he was wearing a white shirt or light coloured, and a tie ... Would have been about 5'11" or 5'10" [180 or 179 cm] ... Round about 25.

A person familiar with beats and beat behaviour would be aware of the dual dangers: being attacked by a youth or a gang of youths, or being entrapped or assaulted by one or more Vice Squad officers. James had identified a man who was formally dressed in a full suit with tie, and later recalls his impression that the attackers 'were all wearing suits, or coats of some sort'. This is not the clothing young gay bashers would be expected to be wearing; it is far more likely to be the attire of Vice Squad officers. Yet James expresses surprise when at the police station three men are shown separately to him – presumably all wearing suits – before one of them refers to the inspector as 'sir'. James says he thinks he is being tricked, but this can only be on the basis that he has not even conceived the possibility that his attackers were policemen. For a person who knows how beats operate and, in particular, the No. 1 Beat, this is difficult to believe. As a July 1972 story in the *Review* reported: 'Vice Squad activity at Adelaide's beats has been of such a vicious intensity over a long period of time, that stories constantly circulate amongst homosexuals about these confrontations.'

James' level of accuracy about clothing is also surprising given how unclear he was about how many people were involved

The Death of Dr Duncan

in the attack. When he was interviewed by the *Advertiser* the day before the inquest, he said there were three men who were dragging Duncan down – making a total of four attackers. Yet at the inquest it was firstly 'a group of people' around Duncan, then 'I'd say about three', then 'more than one, could be two or more' who attacked him, and then 'I didn't really notice how many there were' as the attackers initially moved away. He settled on four in total, seemingly after he identified that number of people who later crossed Victoria Drive into Kintore Avenue. But when he was later recalled he admitted that there were 'more than two, but I can't say how many' in describing the group around Duncan.

It could be argued that problems of identification were due, in part, to the fact that two lights close to the scene were not working on the night of the drowning. James did indeed claim that 'it was too dark to see the men clearly'. However, the New Scotland Yard detectives re-examined the conditions that night, including the weather ('calm with low cloud'), temperature (16 °C) and visibility ('good'). They contended that the street lighting from Victoria Drive reflected onto the paths by the river. Their conclusion: 'The conditions existing in the area on this particular evening were such that if any person were close enough they would be easily recognisable.'

James claimed at the inquest that he received a blow to the head before he was thrown into the river. He broke his ankle

The Drowning

and probably was in acute shock in the cold water. When the attackers returned as James was pulling himself out of the river, at least one (again James was unsure) pushed him back in. Yet he was not asked at the inquest why, at such close range, he didn't see one or more of their faces. At the point when one of the group dived in to try and find Duncan, James stated that one of the attackers 'helped me out of the water'. Yet he was not urged to explain why he could not identify this person. More than this, he said: 'I did see all [the attackers'] faces as I lay on the bank but I can't remember now.' This was the most crucial admission of all, particularly as it confirmed that the fact the lights were not working had not impaired his ability to see, but no further clarification was sought. He *had* seen the attackers' faces so he knew their number and what they looked like; why could he not remember? Was he in shock or was there another reason?

In the earlier *National U* story, Mr P claimed that 'James said he was stoned on the night'. As noted, James claimed that this and other newspaper articles of the time contained statements that were 'vicious lies'. But a 1987 Abuse of Process application to the Supreme Court (in the lead-up to the 1988 trial) revealed that James had told his inquest lawyer, Garry Hiskey, that he had taken drugs on the day of the death. He said he shared a joint with the friend with whom he later had dinner, as well as taking hashish, which gave him a four-hour high. In the 1980

Empire Times story, however, James admitted that there was a 'heavy session of marijuana smoking' followed by a late dinner where wine was consumed. The article stated: 'The marijuana and the wine had combined to make [James] feel very stoned.'

This may explain why James was slow to react in the build-up to the attack when, as someone experienced in beat behaviour, he should have been aware of the unfolding danger. The man who propositioned him was using the crass argot of a decoy policeman; James said 'he certainly wasn't a homosexual ... I feel he was too aggressive'. Meanwhile, the group approaching from the left was trapping him in a pincer movement with – it is suggested to James at the inquest by Bruce Debelle, counsel representing the University of Adelaide – Duncan 'walking unwillingly or being pushed along'. James concedes: 'I'd say, yes, I suppose.' It is difficult for him to acknowledge the reality of the situation because he has insisted he is there that night innocently. Of course, he has undermined his position by confessing he knew that the man who was conversing with him was not homosexual. But he is also stoned when, as will be seen, he was on a bond for drug offences.

However, even if James were stoned and/or drunk and/or in shock, it is difficult to understand how he saw and was able to describe things that night – and at a distance – with absolute clarity. Von Einem testified at the inquest that James told him in the car 'about this man going into the water with his hands above the water and him going under the water and disappearing'. During the 2005 ABC television interview, James said he was able to see – and Duncan was 3.7 metres from the bank – that his body 'just slipped away, and the water just rippled back again'. At the inquest James had also said that, after crawling with his broken ankle, he later saw four people cross into Victoria Drive. He said the driver of the car had a white shirt on, not a coat, and was the person who had first spoken to him. He also described the coat of one of the men: 'A sports coat, a tweed fabric with a check in it.' He even posited that the car was a 'fairly new looking' white Valiant. There was so much acute and detailed recollection of things far away, but no detail close by. His main recall was that the attackers were all aged in the vicinity of 25 and one had blond hair; he also loosely described their physical build. But he was unclear about their exact number and he had virtually no memory for faces.

In the *National U* story Mr P claimed: 'Well, according to Bevan [von Einem], James said to him that it was the police who did it.' When the interviewee asked, 'Why didn't James say this?' Mr P responded: 'He is on a two years drug bond.' The New Scotland Yard report confirmed that James had appeared at the Adelaide Magistrates Court on 18 November 1971 – roughly six months before the death – on charges of possessing Indian hemp and a pipe for smoking it. He had been sentenced to three months' imprisonment, which was suspended, and placed on a bond for *three* years. In the *Advertiser* James denounced this and related stories:

> The author of some of these statements claim that I have spoken in confidence about the Duncan case to a number of unnamed persons in Adelaide and have, among other things, positively identified the men who attacked Dr Duncan and myself on the night of 10 May. It has also been alleged that I have failed to reveal all I know to the police through fear of reprisals by them in relation to drug offences. These statements are vicious lies. I wish to make it clear that I have told the police and the Coroner's Court everything I know.

Yet James had not revealed the true state of his connection with von Einem. At the inquest von Einem stated he had never before seen James. James likewise described von Einem only as a 'passing motorist'; he was not asked but did not volunteer information about possibly knowing him. This position was maintained at the 2005 television interview. But at the 1988 trial it had been reported by the *News* and the *Advertiser* that James admitted that they did know each other, if only on the beat. Of course, if von Einem not only was known but was another gay man – and one who also did the beats and knew the risks of police entrapment – then it would not be inconceivable for James to make statements to him about what had just occurred, including alleged culpability in the drowning.

The Drowning

Roger James was terrorised and brutalised on the night of the attack. He suffered the horrifying ordeal of being pushed into the water twice, of breaking an ankle as well as watching a man drown when – because of his own injury – he was unable to assist him. He crawled away from the attackers, believing they would return to kill him as the sole witness. And as will be revealed in the next chapter, the police handling of a line-up had the potential to terrorise James even further. The trauma of that night cannot have been lessened by what followed in the months afterward, and in subsequent years when he was required to give evidence at a preliminary hearing and trial.

There were many other people on the riverbank that night, however, so much so that someone later described it as being 'like Rundle Mall'. It is now necessary to examine how the early police investigation dealt with the multitude of witnesses.

PART II
THE DUNCAN CASE

POLICE QUESTIONED OVER RIVER DEATH

By BOB WHITINGTON

Three vice squad police have been questioned by senior police officials about a man who died after having allegedly been thrown into the River Torrens on May 10.

Homicide squad detectives are investigating the death of University of Adelaide law lecturer Dr. George Ian Duncan, 42, of Lincoln College, North Adelaide.

A high-ranking police officer confirmed last night that the policemen had been questioned with a number of other people.

He said enquiries were continuing.

Dr. Duncan and Mr. Roger Wesley James, 27, of Prospect road, Fitzroy, were reported to have been thrown into the River Torrens, near the University of Adelaide footbridge, shortly before 11 p.m. on May 10.

A check at Mr. James's home last night revealed he had left for Sydney yesterday morning.

The house was dark and the blinds were drawn.

A neighbor, who did not want his name published, said Mr. James had come to his home on Thursday to say goodbye, and had said he was leaving the next day for Sydney.

Mr. James, who was admitted to the Royal Adelaide Hospital with a broken ankle after the incident, is reported to have told detectives that a group of young men had thrown Dr. Duncan and himself into the river.

He said one of the attackers had stripped to the waist and plunged into the river in an unsuccessful attempt to find Dr. Duncan.

He said the attackers fled from the scene and drove off in a car.

Describing the incident, Mr. James is reported to have told police that the young men came up to Dr. Duncan and himself and said to Dr. Duncan: "How would you like a swim?" and pushed him backwards into the river.

A similar remark was made to Mr. James and he said he also was pushed backwards into the river.

Senior police inspectors brought into the enquiry were told that two members of the vice squad had been down to the vicinity when they visited a lavatory near the City Bridge because one of them had felt sick.

They had been driving home from a party, held after a Vietnam veterans' march in which the sick man inhaled fumes from a bomb.

It is understood that certain police officers, acting on legal advice, declined to appear in a police line up and at least one refused to answer questions.

However, three police officers were viewed by Mr. James individually and he is reported to have said they were not the men that had assaulted him.

Police are puzzled that nobody has come forward who might be a relative of Dr. Duncan.

A note found in his room at Lincoln College stated that if anything happened to him a firm of solicitors in Melbourne was to be contacted.

Police contacted this firm and were told that an Adelaide firm of solicitors would act in the case.

So far no firm has contacted police.

It is understood that Mr. James had decided to go to Sydney before the date of the incident.

The Commissioner of Police (Mr. J. G. McKinna) said last night he knew nothing about the matter.

He said he would not comment.

Advertiser story, 20 May 1972

CHAPTER 4
Police Investigation

On 20 May – 10 days after the death – the *Advertiser* updated the Duncan case but this time it was a front-page story: 'Police Questioned Over River Death'. A woman had rung the newsroom with an anonymous tipoff that three officers had been arrested, but she was wrong. A 'high-ranking police officer' confirmed to the paper that three Vice Squad officers had been questioned. The story continued:

> It is understood that certain police officers, acting on legal advice, declined to appear in a police line-up and at least one refused to answer questions. However, three police officers were viewed by Mr James individually and he is reported to have said they were not the men that had assaulted him.

The Police Commissioner, John McKinna, issued a statement in response declaring that 'at the moment there is nothing to implicate any policemen with the death of Dr George Duncan'.

McKinna's statement concealed the fact that, from 13 to 17 May, a series of interviews had been held with two Vice Squad officers who were in the area around the time of the attack – but had not reported it. Those officers were Constables Francis

The Death of Dr Duncan

John Cawley and Michael Kenneth Clayton. They had attended a send-off that night at the King's Head Hotel for a colleague, Constable Edwin Mildenhall, who was leaving the force. Clayton earlier that day had policed an anti-Vietnam war demonstration and inhaled fumes from a smoke bomb. He had collapsed and, having been revived by an ambulance, returned to his duties. Now, having left the send-off with Cawley and while travelling down King William Road – at about 10.30 pm he told his superiors – he had felt sick and they had pulled into Victoria Drive so he could vomit in the men's toilet.

McKinna had appointed Inspectors Colin Lehmann and Paul Turner – two independent officers of the Criminal Investigation Bureau who were not connected with the Vice Squad – to oversee the investigation. They both interviewed Cawley:

Q: You know or you have heard, that around 11 or shortly before that evening two men were thrown into the river at a spot east of the police station by four men, and as a result one man suffered a broken ankle and the other man drowned?

A: I have heard that.

Q: It would therefore appear that you and Clayton were in the vicinity of this happening at around the time it happened.

A: I don't know exactly what time this happened.

Q: If I was to tell you that it happened about 11 o'clock or

Police Investigation

shortly before, would you agree that you would have been in the vicinity at about that time?

A: Not at 11 o'clock, sir.

Q: Didn't the fact that a man was drowned near where you had been that evening give you some reason to consider that you might have been some help in the investigation?

A: I agree with that, sir.

Q: Did you make a report or inform anyone that you were down around there at about this time?

A: No, sir.

Q: That was rather unusual, wasn't it?

A: I didn't think I could help at all, sir.

Cawley was pressed further:

Q: Since you have been on the Vice Squad have you paid continual or fairly close attention to this area of the River Torrens regarding homosexuals?

A: Yes, sir ...

Q: How many people have you reported in connection with homosexuality in this area?

A: I couldn't say, sir. It would be a fair few.

Q: Do you believe that the homosexual activities down there warrant strict police supervision?

A: Yes, sir.

Q: Are these your own thoughts on the matter or are these instructions you have received from a senior officer?

A: Earlier there were instructions received, but recently in my mind I believe that they should be policed strictly.

Q: Would you say that you are biased against people with homosexual tendencies?

A: No, sir.

Q: Have you ever heard of any homosexuals being thrown into the river?

A: No, sir.

Clayton initially stated that he and Cawley had spent around 10 minutes on the river that night, but this was challenged when it was revealed that a uniformed officer on duty claimed to have spoken to Cawley at around 10.55 pm. Clayton was interviewed by Turner:

Q: You did not mention to any members of the Homicide Squad that you were in the area that evening and could perhaps help their investigation?

A: I didn't think of it...

Q: You saw quite a bit that night, didn't you?

A: Not anything very much.

Police Investigation

The suspicion of Cawley's and Clayton's involvement spread to a third policeman, Senior Constable Brian Edwin Hudson, who was interviewed on 16 May. Hudson was new to the Vice Squad, having only joined two months earlier. He was also, aged 37, older than his colleagues who were in their early to mid-20s. He had been at the police farewell too but was circumspect when asked about his movements thereafter. Hudson claimed that his inspectors were 'talking to me about a serious matter and I feel I should seek advice from a solicitor'. He returned soon after and stated that he had been advised not to make a statement. He declined to answer questions at another interview the following day, as did Cawley and Clayton. All three officers also declined to participate in a formal police line-up, but agreed to be shown individually to James.

This unusual state of affairs was criticised by a colleague of the three Vice Squad officers, Michael (Mick) O'Shea, after he came forward in 1985 with claims of a police cover-up. O'Shea stated that police protocol dictated that a line-up should only occur under certain conditions, including that there be at least eight persons of similar appearance to the suspect:

> What it does is it disqualifies that witness from being a credible witness because they've tainted him. They've got one offender standing in a room and you're supposed to have eight if you want a positive ID. If [James] had said, 'It's definitely him,' [this would be] inadmissible – inadmissible

because in obtaining that evidence of positive ID it is completely in breach of the rules of evidence and the rules of court.

It also allowed Cawley, Clayton and Hudson to be at very close quarters with the sole witness to the drowning. It would not be unreasonable for a witness in such a situation to feel intimidated – even terrified – especially when he is viewing not one but three possible suspects, and he is not protected by anonymity. Added to this, it is occurring at police headquarters. It happened not only to James but also Kevin Williamson, who ended up perjuring himself.

On 17 May Roger James was brought into SA Police. His leg was still in plaster; he was made to wait and forced to stand during identification. The three Vice Squad officers were then each brought in and taken out again: Cawley, Hudson, then Clayton. James was now face-to-face with the possible killers of Duncan and his own attackers. He asked Cawley to speak and to turn around, and then said: 'No, I haven't seen him before.' His response was the same with Clayton. The experience with Hudson, however, was different. James also decided he was unable to identify him, but Hudson said words to the effect of: 'I have seen this man before.' James said that Hudson then added: 'I'll speak to you afterwards.'

Police Investigation

James reported that he advised Lehmann that he could not understand Hudson's comments which Lehmann presumably, and unaccountably, took at face value. Where had Hudson seen James before: at the beat, during his arrest for possession of drugs, or in another potentially compromising situation? Hudson said he couldn't recall. But if it did involve possible criminal behaviour, then surely the statement that followed could be interpreted as a veiled threat? The exchange was raised at the inquest but was not pursued further, yet it raised the possibility that James surreptitiously had been warned to keep quiet. Is this the reason for James' later improbable narrative, that he didn't even know he was being shown policemen?

On 19 May Hudson made a formal – if grammatically sloppy – statement to his superiors:

> Regarding my movements on the night of May 10, I now wish to state that after attending a function at the King's Head Hotel, King William Street, Adelaide, I am unable to assist with the matter of a person being drowned in the River Torrens on that date.
>
> Because of rumours concerning me, the reason of my not appearing in a police line-up was on the advice of my solicitor who considered that this would not be in my best interests because I have attended toilets situated at Victoria Drive, Adelaide, on numerous occasions as a police officer on duty.

The Death of Dr Duncan

The following day Cawley and Clayton also produced statements denying any connection with the drowning, and confirming that they may be targeted by people with a grudge against them if they appeared in a line-up.

The police released Duncan's body for burial, but on condition it not be cremated. The funeral was paid for by the Public Trustee in South Australia, which was now handling the estate. The funeral directors had proposed a short service at their parlour, but Professor Lücke deemed this 'indifferent' and the Requiem Mass followed. Burial was in the Anglican section of Centennial Park Cemetery, with the grave headed by a black-granite tombstone that read: 'Endowed With Modesty and Scholarship'.

On 27 May the full implications of the Duncan case came into sharp focus – and not just in South Australia – with a full-page story in the *Review*, a left-leaning national newspaper. This identified the place of murder as a well-known beat and revealed for the first time the darker side of police harassment of homosexuals, particularly in their use of *agents provocateurs* in entrapment. It even claimed that there was one policeman in Adelaide who had homosexual intercourse and then arrested his sexual partner. But it also blamed gangs of young men for being 'poofter bashers'. It asked why James had 'disappeared' and identified him as 'Dr Duncan's companion'. It stated that the number plate of the vehicle in which the killers escaped

Police Investigation

Ian Duncan's tombstone

had been identified as an unmarked police car. It criticised McKinna's statement, calling for the investigation to be taken out of the hands of the police and suggesting the establishment of a royal commission. It also argued for the decriminalisation of male homosexual acts. Its final exhortation: 'Your move, Donny, Mr Premier.' It was a provocative and powerful piece written by an unnamed 'Adelaide correspondent'.

The *Review* story was not taken up by the *Advertiser*. It was only on 5 June that the newspaper reported that 'members of the homicide squad have made extensive enquiries among Adelaide's homosexual community'. But the local gay community group CAMP was as much in the dark as anyone else. One member recalled: 'We were picking up the same fragments ... reading the same newspapers. None of us knew Dr Duncan.'

It was Duncan's head of department, Professor Horst Lücke, who acted by writing to Commissioner McKinna, who was about to be replaced by Harold Salisbury. Lücke had heard, after someone in the police had spoken out of turn, that 'the autopsy report contained statements involving Dr Duncan's moral character'. It says something of the tenor of the time that he was alluding to the report's pathological references to Duncan's homosexuality, which would be brought to the fore during the inquest. Lücke's explosive letter was copied to the Chief Secretary and Attorney-General, and published in the press. It appeared together with a front-page story in the *Advertiser*:

> Your own comments ... may have reassured some members of the public that the police were not implicated. However, I should have been more completely reassured had you adverted specifically to the most disturbing of all the circumstances surrounding the case, i.e. the refusal of several policemen to join a police line-up and the refusal of at least one to answer questions. Although such conduct is not incompatible with innocence, it is also surely indicative of the fear on the part of the persons involved that any evidence their co-operation

Police Investigation

might bring to light would point in their direction. In these circumstances, what steps are being taken to reassure the public of the integrity of the Police Force?

Lücke also said that the departure of James was regarded by a number of people as 'strange', and asked what steps were being taken to ensure he would make himself available as a witness if required. The reply from SA Police, also published in the *Advertiser*, stated that 'no particular classes or sections of the community will receive any special treatment in the pursuit of our enquiries'. It also concluded with the frank admission: 'At this stage of our enquiry there is certainly no evidence to connect any particular person or persons with this offence.' This was a dramatic turnaround from the newspaper story less than two weeks earlier, which had stated that Vice Squad officers had been questioned over Duncan's death.

When Lücke later briefed the Vice-Chancellor he explained his actions thus:

> Before writing I sought the advice of two persons whose judgement I have come to respect greatly and they both thought the letter should be written. I wrote it ... but did not in any way seek the publicity which was given it.

Its impact was aided by an *Advertiser* editorial which stated that there was 'a feeling abroad that investigations into Dr Duncan's death have not been pressed with sufficient vigor'.

This was a bold move by the newspaper and raised the stakes for the government.

Attorney-General Len King responded by calling for a full report from the Police Commissioner. This was completed by Lehmann and Turner but not released publicly. It was signed off by Lehmann as the superior officer. It concluded:

> This report covers the extent of the enquiry into Dr Duncan's death and the assault on James to this date. Other enquiries have been conducted by members of the Homicide Squad into the activities of groups of youths who have, on previous occasions, allegedly thrown homosexuals into the Torrens.
>
> In the opinion of the pathologist who conducted the autopsy on the dead man, Duncan was a passive homosexual. Although James denied being a homosexual to the investigating officers, he had in October last year, when charged with drug offences, admitted to the police that he was a homosexual. The presence of both men on the banks of the Torrens at this time would tend to substantiate his evidence. The evidence so far in this matter suggests that there may be other people who were present on the riverbank that evening and who may have important information to give the police. The fact that no one has come forward so far indicates either they saw nothing or that they are homosexuals who fear their activities and or deviations may become public knowledge. Enquiries will be assiduously continued with the view to the eventual apprehension of the offenders.

Police Investigation

Govt. calls for facts in Duncan case

Mr. King

The Attorney-General (Mr. King) has called for a report on the progress of police investigations into the death of a university lecturer.

Mr. King said yesterday he had asked for the report in view of publicity the matter had received and certain suggestions which had been made about the case.

He said he considered it was necessary for him to be told of the progress of the investigations.

Earlier yesterday, letters dealing with the case or the head of the Department of Law at the University of Adelaide (Professor H. K. Lucke) and the Chief of the CIB (Superintendent N. R. Lenton) were released.

Professor Lucke

Superintendent Lenton said in his letter to Professor Lucke that the Government had called for "a full report."

Dr. George Ian Duncan, 42, a lecturer at the University of Adelaide Law School, was allegedly pushed into the River Torrens on the night of May 10.

Professor Lucke announced on Sunday that he was writing to the Commissioner of Police (Mr. J. G. McKinna) about Dr. Duncan's death.

Professor Lucke said then that he would not release details of his letter until Mr. McKinna had had a chance to read it.

Yesterday Professor Lucke gave copies of his letter and a reply from Superintendent Lenton, on behalf of Mr. McKinna, to the Press.

"The Advertiser" revealed on May 20 that members of the Adelaide CIB vice squad had been questioned about the death of Dr. Duncan.

Superintendent Lenton

Attorney-General Len King acts

To date there is no evidence to substantiate a charge against any person or persons for this offence.

Lehmann had revealed that police were well aware that James was homosexual. Lehmann had also identified a crucial point: homosexual witnesses were fearful of coming forward, an issue which would become more pressing as the case progressed. It is not clear if his reference to 'deviations' was simply the use of accepted police terminology or a sign of ingrained homophobia. When Lehmann was interviewed for a

1993 ABC television story, he was asked if it was fairly common practice in 1972 for police officers to throw homosexuals into the River Torrens. He responded: 'Homosexuals were being ill-treated and bashed around ... by all sorts of gangs.' He said the Duncan case was used to undermine the integrity and authority of SA Police, and that claims of a police cover-up 'was a lot of rot', adding: 'If there was any cover-up being done it was done by the homosexual people.' But the reopening of the case eight years earlier that had led to three charges of manslaughter – which will be examined in Chapter 7 – was precisely the result of claims by a former insider of a police cover-up. To blame solely 'the homosexual people', with its attendant emotive language, and when it was a member of this group that had been senselessly killed, was not only misguided but cruel.

Len King read the report and almost immediately – on 2 June – ordered an inquest to be conducted by the City Coroner, Tom Cleland. It was within King's powers as Attorney-General to do so, even before the police investigation was complete. It would be a decision criticised by the New Scotland Yard report.

Henceforward the Duncan case would attract massive media attention. By July the *Advertiser* had devoted to it over 2000 column inches and four feature articles. Over a period of 10 weeks it would appear on the front page of Adelaide's three main newspapers – the *Advertiser*, *News* and *Sunday Mail* – a total of 31 times. The 21 June front-page story in the *Advertiser* even included an aerial photo of the drowning site.

The *Sunday Mail* also ran a major story: 'The Duncan affair – not since the Beaumont case has the South Australian public been confronted with a puzzle so baffling, so mysterious and so rumour-prone.' It seemed hyperbolic to compare the Duncan case to the still unsolved 1966 disappearance of the three Beaumont children in Adelaide. The article continued: 'One of the more extreme rumours surrounding the case appeared in the *Review*. It suggested a police officer committed offences in order to apprehend homosexuals.' The outgoing Police Commissioner, John McKinna, responded that the charge had been thoroughly investigated and was a 'total fabrication'.

But the case was out of the hands of the police. It was now the responsibility of the coroner.

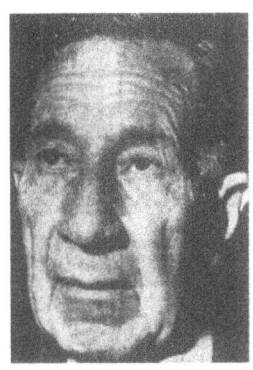

City Coroner Tom Cleland

CHAPTER 5
Coroner's Inquest

The inquest began on 7 June, exactly four weeks after Duncan's death. It would sit nine times until the coroner's findings were delivered on 5 July. City Coroner Tom Cleland had held the position since 1947 and was aged 78. The Crown Solicitor had appointed Rod Matheson as counsel assisting the coroner; Bruce Debelle appeared for the University of Adelaide and to protect the interests of Dr Duncan. Both would be future judges of the Supreme Court of South Australia. The key witness, Roger James, was also represented by counsel – Garry Hiskey – though, as James pointed out, it was an expense he could ill-afford when he was unemployed. He had been summonsed to appear from his new Sydney address where he was located by an *Advertiser* journalist. He reiterated that he did not know Duncan and described the drowning as 'a terrible accident'.

On the opening day of the inquest CAMP claimed it had interviewed three men who wished to give evidence but were reluctant to 'because their homosexual activities could be disclosed to their employers, parents and friends'. One of the men claimed to have taken the registration number of a car he thought belonged to the police, and said that of four men he saw that night he believed one was 'vice squad decoy for homosexuals'. Then a further witness was reported as refusing to go to the police for fear of repercussions. Premier Don Dunstan was forced to step in, promising government protection, including full anonymity and immunity 'from any prosecution for any personal activities as a homosexual'. He added: 'If it can be established that "poofter bashing" goes on in South Australia, we will not allow it to continue.' Two days later the second Duncan editorial in the *Advertiser* would

The Duncan inquest

The inquest into the death of Dr. George Duncan involves something quite different from most other inquests. The known facts and the air of mystery which has descended upon them have made this an exceptional case. Apart from the strange circumstances surrounding the death of Dr. Duncan, the affair has raised questions concerning members of the Police Force, and has also touched upon the broader issue of homosexuality and attitudes towards it in our society. For all these reasons, it is important that the inquest be able to determine the true circumstances surrounding the death.

To do this, it is vitally important that everyone who may be able to help comes forward. However, one of the most unfortunate aspects of this case is that some people who might be able to help have not come forward. In particular, it is believed that there were witnesses to Dr. Duncan's death who are now reluctant to talk to police because they may be called homosexuals and are afraid of this being disclosed.

In these circumstances, it is only sensible of the Premier (Mr. Dunstan) to offer Government protection to those who are afraid to give evidence. As a result, it has been suggested that some evidence could be given in camera when the inquest resumes on Friday. Regrettable as it is, such a restriction on the public's right to know what is going on seems necessary.

At the same time, however, the nature of that restriction should be kept to a minimum. While there are good grounds for protecting some witnesses, the rights of the public must also be remembered. It is not difficult to see how the interests of both parties can be balanced, perhaps by closing the inquest to all but the Press and, even then, concealing the identities of certain witnesses.

Every effort must be made to clear the uneasy atmosphere which surrounds the Duncan affair, but it would be most unfortunate if those efforts were to result in the intrusion of an unwarranted degree of secrecy into proceedings.

THOUGHT FOR TODAY — *And Jesus came and touched them and said, Be not afraid.*
—*Matthew 17:7*

Advertiser editorial

make an important, tentative link by stating that the affair had 'touched upon the broader issue of homosexuality and attitudes towards it in our society'.

Duncan's boss Horst Lücke attended every hearing. The courtroom in Waymouth Street only had room for 35 people and was overflowing on the first day. James was the star witness but his evidence, including under sustained cross-examination, was that he could not definitively identify the attackers. He was followed by the pathologist, Dr Colin Manock, who concluded from the autopsy – and which the coroner accepted – that Dr Duncan was a homosexual. Manock's report, which was tendered into evidence, stated:

> Rectum was healthy. The anus was lax and the normal folds of the anal sphincter were poorly defined. The anus was generally funnel-shaped and had the appearance of that of a passive homosexual [who engages in receptive anal intercourse].

This was all too much for the *Advertiser* which could not bring itself to describe Duncan's anal characteristics. Manock's statement was exacerbated when he was later recalled for he claimed that due to Duncan's circumcision and extended submersion in the water, it was not possible to determine whether he had been an active homosexual (who engages in penetrative anal intercourse) that night. These declarations combined with James' evidence of being asked 'Do you take it or give it?' to portray homosexuality as relating narrowly to sexual activity, and specifically anal sex.

Manock was Director of Forensic Pathology in the state. Legal academic Dr Robert Moles has shown how Manock's autopsy findings variously have been harshly criticised by the coroner, found wanting by a royal commission, and led to a conviction for attempted murder being overturned by the High Court. A recent case to have directly challenged Manock's conclusions is that of Henry Keogh. Moles, however, has not reported on the Duncan case.

The linking of homosexuality with anal and other defects was first made in a mid-19th century book by a French doctor, Auguste-Ambroise Tardieu. Like Duncan, Tardieu is also to be found in the *Who's Who in Gay & Lesbian History*, but for all the wrong reasons. According to him passive homosexuals had buttocks that were 'wide, protruding, often enormous and entirely feminine in shape', as well as the aforementioned funnel-shaped anus. Active homosexuals had a dog-like or club-shaped penis. Men who practised oral sex had crooked mouths, short teeth and thick lips. This archaic thinking, which equated homosexuality with deformed physiology, was never questioned and became the accepted wisdom about Duncan's sexuality. Possibly this is what Manock was taught in medical school but, as student journalist Paul Foss asserted, it was 'chilling to realise that the law can accept the definition of homosexuality in purely pathological terms'.

On the inquest's second sitting day Kevin Williamson gave startling evidence. He had been at an event at the Torrens Parade Ground before crossing Victoria Drive to sit on a bench on the upper path and smoke a cigarette. It was close to the time of the attack on Duncan and James. He saw four men run past on the lower path before stopping; two of them then approached him separately. The first said: 'Best get out of here, the coppers will be here shortly.' Only after a second, more aggressive, man warded him off did Williamson agree to move; he returned to his car. Williamson claimed to see the four men later cross into Victoria Drive, confirming James' evidence (it seemed unusual that Williamson and James had not seen each other, but James was sheltering under a pine tree before moving to the roadside to be rescued). But what made no sense was Williamson's claim that, when sitting in his car, he was able to see people walking on the lower path – for he should have witnessed the attack. The steepness of the bank as it descended toward the river made this a physical impossibility, but he was not challenged on this point.

Matheson questioned Williamson in an attempt to identify the men who had approached him:

Q: Have a look at the two men on the back seat and man sitting on the front seat and tell His Honour if you've ever seen these men before today.

A: No, I haven't.

Q: Quite sure neither one or more of those three spoke to you when you were sitting on the bench on the night in question?

A: Quite sure.

Williamson had just perjured himself; he had also lied in an early police line-up. As he later admitted to the New Scotland Yard detectives, he easily recognised Senior Constable Hudson as the first man who addressed him that night and Constable Clayton as the second. But his evidence, and his credibility, could now be called into doubt.

Three homosexual witnesses had come forward under protection of anonymity (which still operates). They were identified as Witnesses B, C and D and represented in court by Robyn Layton, another future judge of the Supreme Court. They all told of sitting in a parked car on Victoria Drive on the night and watching a group of men running around and fighting (it could have been play-fighting, they said) among the boatsheds close to City Bridge. They flashed their car headlights to illuminate the goings-on and even went for several walks to investigate. It is unknown if these were the witnesses who were reported in a student newspaper as saying that Duncan and James were involved in the fighting, before being dragged down to the riverbank. In any event this was not evidence they gave at the inquest.

One of the witnesses had identified at police headquarters one of the men whom he saw that night as Cawley. Another officer was identified as being seen twice that night, including earlier in the evening and, strangely, when wearing a silver lamé jacket. It was Hudson, who was then questioned by Inspector Lehmann. 'I have been advised by my solicitor not to answer any further questions regarding this matter,' responded Hudson. 'But he is very wrong, Inspector.'

These witnesses noticed a car pull up that they believed was used by Vice Squad police in their activities entrapping homosexual men at the beat. It transpired that the car belonged to another mystery witness – Witness A, otherwise known as 'Mr X' – who came forward with shocking new evidence. Mr X was represented at the inquest by Derrance Stevenson who, in another twist in the Duncan case, would himself be killed by his young male lover in 1979 in Adelaide's infamous 'Body in the Freezer' case.

Mr X – whose identity also is still protected – was married with children but living a double life. He only gave evidence after police traced his car. About half an hour before the main attack he entered the toilet block on Victoria Drive where he engaged a man in conversation. He returned to his car, drove off then saw the man again walking beside the road. Mr X pulled over and followed him to the steps close to where Duncan and James were thrown in, when a second man suddenly appeared. The attack on Mr X was particularly brutal:

> I was pushed or thrown down the steps. I think I landed about halfway, then I'm not too sure of the details, but I think when I got to my feet the two men followed me the rest of the way down the steps. I landed on the path at the bottom ... I got to my feet and started going up the steps again, the men disappeared out of immediate range at that stage ... then they rushed in again and threw me down the steps ... I think I was trying to get to my feet and the two men rushed, one from either side, and said something like, 'I hope you can swim' or 'I hope you like swimming' and picked me up and threw me into the river.

These words were almost identical to those James said were spoken by the attackers as Duncan was tossed in. Mr X was aware of the silhouette of a third man standing under a tree before all three departed via the lower path in a westerly direction toward City Bridge. After getting out of the river he drove round to dry his clothes off, before later burning them. He suffered physical injuries and took time off work. He admitted he had not immediately reported the attack to police as 'I've been in trouble before', when he was convicted for loitering in

The Death of Dr Duncan

Stairs where Mr X was attacked

the South Park Lands. He acknowledged he was frightened of the police. Even when he stated that the lighting in the toilet was 'good', and that when he caught up with the first man he was only 20 feet (6 m) away from the well-lit Victoria Drive, he was unable positively to identify any of the three men. He said he thought the first man was Cawley, but couldn't be sure, though he was formally attired in a coat.

Another man who claimed to have had a similar experience that night – though not as vicious – was Robert Osborne, who came forward late in the piece. Osborne acknowledged at the inquest that he was a homosexual, after being asked by Matheson. This was a risky admission and Mr X's lawyer objected on his behalf as Osborne was unrepresented. He was advised by the coroner that he could refuse to answer any questions on the grounds of possible self-incrimination. Osborne responded: 'I signed a statement so ... I have to stick by it.' In an incredible coincidence, his job was as a car washer with the police force, from which he resigned once he decided to give evidence. He had only been educated to Grade 3 and could read printing but not writing.

Osborne said that he was doing the No. 1 Beat on the night of 10 May, but had departed the scene before the attack on Duncan and James. He had also been in the toilet and been approached by a man – whom he had seen on the beat several weeks earlier – and then been chased by him after rejecting his advances. Osborne made the astonishing claim that he had locked himself in his car while the man banged on the roof with his fists. Osborne then drove away and was followed down Kintore Avenue by the man with three others in another car. His story had so many similarities with earlier evidence, but there were other elements that were unconvincing and his inability to be accurate about timing must have cast doubt on his credibility. The coroner in his summary referenced only the quarrel and chase from the toilet, without alluding to other details of the testimony. Osborne also failed to feature in the New Scotland Yard report.

However, evidence was emerging – and from other police officers – which highlighted the alleged activities of Cawley that night. Constables Darryl Smedley and Martin Maynard were on duty, and in uniform, and had parked their car on the southern side of Victoria Drive close to King William Road. They were taking a break, watching an army band at the Torrens Parade Ground. At between 10.20 and 10.30 pm they became aware of a man approaching the left-hand side of their car. It was Cawley, who said words to the effect of: 'Would you mind taking a drive, you are buggering up our poofters on the river.' As the constables departed, they claimed they noticed Cawley crossing Victoria Drive heading in the direction of the toilets.

Constable Ronald Harris also made astounding revelations. He was on uniform duty as well that night but was based at the police station close to Victoria Drive, a short walk from where Duncan and James were attacked. He was descending the stairs from City Bridge when he recognised Cawley coming up. Harris also noticed a person at the bottom of the stairway whom he assumed was with Cawley, but could not identify him. Harris was questioned by Coroner Cleland:

Q: What did you say to him?

A: Just as he was stepping past me on the steps I said: 'Good day, John.'

Q: What did he say?

A: He said: 'Fuck off, fuck off.'

Harris was cross-examined:

Q: You said when Mr Cawley spoke to you, you thought there may have been a person or persons under observation at the toilets?

A: This is the impression I formed.

Q: Why did this request give you that impression?

A: His request sounded somewhat anxious.

On 29 June Clayton became the first of the three Vice Squad officers linked to the affair to take to the stand. All three would be represented by the same counsel, Bob McRae. Clayton's records of interviews with Inspectors Lehmann and Turner, and his own statement to them, were admitted into evidence. He was questioned by Matheson who asked if Clayton had left the party at the King's Head Hotel with Cawley. Clayton declined to answer on the grounds it may incriminate him. Matheson persisted:

> Q: Did you accompany another police officer to the vicinity of the men's toilet near the City Bridge after leaving the party?
>
> A: I decline to answer on the grounds that it may tend to incriminate me.
>
> Q: Were you in fact sick in the men's toilet on Victoria Drive in the vicinity of Torrens Bridge?
>
> A: I refuse to answer on the grounds that it may tend to incriminate me.
>
> Q: Were you present when Dr Duncan and Mr James were thrown into the river?
>
> A: I decline to answer that question on the grounds that it may tend to incriminate me.
>
> Q: Did you see Constable Cawley after you left the party at the King's Head Hotel?
>
> A: I decline to answer that question on the grounds that it may tend to incriminate me.
>
> Q: Did you see Senior Constable Hudson after you left the party at the King's Head Hotel on the night in question?
>
> A: I decline to answer on the grounds it may tend to incriminate me.

Coroner's Inquest

The coroner assumed the questioning. He asked Clayton: 'Do you remember Inspector Lehmann asking you: "Did anyone suggest at the King's Head party that they go down and harass the homosexuals?"' And then: 'Did you say to Inspectors Lehmann and Turner: "There was some talk about homos but not about harassing them?"' Clayton declined to answer.

Cawley's time on the stand was brief for many questions put to him were met with a similar response to Clayton's. The following day – 30 June – all three officers were suspended from their duties. The chief of the Criminal Investigation Bureau, Superintendent Noel Lenton, told them their refusal to answer questions 'reflected discredit on the police force'. Hudson, who also gave evidence that day, promptly resigned, followed by Cawley and Clayton 10 days later. Don Dunstan argued in his political memoirs, *Felicia*, that this was a critical error on the part of the relatively new Police Commissioner, Harold Salisbury:

> Their resignation could have been refused by the Commissioner, and they would still have been subject to police discipline about information. Once out of the force they could stand on their civil rights not to answer questions, and did.

The officers' employment with SA Police, however, did not bind them legally in this way. They may well have been subject to disciplinary procedures but, regardless, they were always within their rights not to answer questions to protect themselves from potential self-incrimination.

Hudson followed Clayton and Cawley on the witness stand. He admitted that he had left the farewell party alone, but declined to provide his car's registration number. Information about his movements thereafter was sought but also was not forthcoming. He was quizzed about his recognition of Roger James at police headquarters but said he was not sure when and where he had seen him. When Debelle asked Hudson about his recent haircut, he declined to answer.

Inspector Turner was the last person called before the inquest. He was cross-examined by Debelle:

Q: Have you asked any police officer other than the three you have referred to, to take part in an identification parade similar to those used to Clayton, Hudson and Cawley?

A: No, other than asking Constable O'Shea was he prepared to allow one witness to view him ...

Q: He did take part in that?

A: Yes.

Q: That was the only occasion anyone has been asked to take part in an identification parade, be it police officer or any other member of the public?

A: That is so.

Coroner's Inquest

Mick O'Shea was the only other Vice Squad officer to have given evidence at the inquest. One of the unnamed witnesses had identified him, but O'Shea had provided an airtight alibi for the time of the drowning. He was not named in the coroner's summary, but for years afterward would be regarded as the mystery 'fourth man' involved in the Duncan case. His story will be examined in more detail in Chapter 7.

The coroner brought down his findings on 5 July. The inquest had taken over 330 pages of evidence and was regarded as 'one of South Australia's longest and most costly'. Before delivering his summary Cleland stated: 'If after giving my finding any information comes forward to the police or me, I think I have the power to open the inquest or the Attorney-General can direct the inquest to be reopened.' But this would never happen.

Cleland's summary was as follows:

Shortly after 11 pm on the 10th May, 1972, Dr Duncan was thrown into the River Torrens, from the southern bank. It was a point north-east from the junction of Victoria Drive and Kintore Avenue and about 370 yards [340 m] from King William Road.

Normally the scene would have been illuminated by two electric lamps, close together. But on this night, and during some previous nights, the lamps were not operating.

Dr Duncan was a homosexual. There is no evidence of his movements during the evening of 10 May. The only evidence is that he was on or near Victoria Drive, and that his car was

The Death of Dr Duncan

parked in King William Road. At the relevant time he may have been coming from, or returning to, his car.

Not long before 10.30 pm two homosexuals quarrelled in a toilet near King William Road. On leaving the toilet one chased the other.

At about this time, according to the evidence of 3 young men sitting in a car, 4 or 5 men were chasing each other around between boat sheds, 70 or 80 yards [64 or 73 m] from King William Road. There was no evidence of the subsequent movements of these men. But while this was going on, they said, a motor car pulled up near them. They said it was a green and white Holden like a police car, and the man who got out of it looked like a plain clothes police officer.

Many questions were put by counsel about this car and man. But after the inquest had proceeded for several days a Mr X came forward and gave evidence. He said that the green and white Holden was his car; that shortly before 10.30 pm he had stopped on the way home to visit the toilet; and that he had visited the toilet. After leaving the toilet he was on the bank of the river, overlooking the place where Dr Duncan was thrown into the water. He was there seized by 2 men, and flung down concrete steps in the river. He incurred some injuries.

The next incident, in point of time, involved a Mr Williamson, who told the police what he knew as soon as he read about Dr Duncan's death, and who gave evidence. He had served in, and retired from, the Regular Army. During the evening of 10 May he was a guest at a Sergeants' Mess on the Parade Ground. He left the Mess at 10.45 pm, walked across the Parade Ground, got some cigarettes from his car, and sat on a seat overlooking the place where Dr Duncan was afterwards thrown into the river. While seated there he was approached by a man who advised him to leave 'before the coppers come'. Mr Williamson did not comply. He was then approached by another man who told him, in more emphatic and somewhat menacing words, to clear out. Mr Williamson thought it wise to do so. He returned to his car, and sat in it, smoking. His car was parked in Victoria Drive close to Kintore Avenue. Some time later he saw 4 men run across Victoria Drive and enter Kintore Avenue. The locality was well lit by three powerful electric lights, and he had a good view of the men.

Not long after Mr Williamson returned to his car, a Mr James was sitting on a seat below the seat on which Mr Williamson had been sitting. A man joined him and made a homosexual inquiry, which Mr James rejected. Four men then appeared on the scene, one of whom turned out to be Dr Duncan. Mr James thought the sound of approaching footsteps were like those of a person walking downhill, or being forced along. At the post-mortem bruises as from fingers were found in the inside of each of Dr Duncan's upper arms, indicating that he was being forced along by men on each side. When the four men were close to Mr James, Dr Duncan was thrown down the bank into the river. Mr James was then seized by two of the men. He resisted, received a blow on the head, and he also was thrown into the river.

The Death of Dr Duncan

Mr James called out that he, i.e. Dr Duncan, was drowning. One of the four men stripped off some clothes, dived into the river, and finally said that he could not find the drowning man.

Meanwhile, Mr James had got out of the river. One of his ankles had been broken. Eventually the four men made off in the direction of Kintore Avenue. Mr James crawled after them. He saw them enter a motor car which was parked in the Avenue, close to Victoria Drive, and drive off to the south.

The next morning, the 11th May, the body of Dr Duncan was found on the bed of the river, in 10 feet [3 m] of water, about 12 feet [3.7 m] from the southern bank, at the place where he was thrown in.

At the direction of the Commissioner of Police, Inspectors Turner and Lehmann made thorough inquiries. They found that two police officers were in the vicinity at times which might have been relevant. These officers were Constables Clayton and Cawley. Each was interrogated by the Inspectors, and a transcript of the questions and answers was received in evidence at this inquest.

It emerged that at a demonstration on the 10th May, Constable Clayton was affected by the smoke of a bomb which struck a man whom he was arresting. During the evening Constables Clayton and Cawley were present at a social function and after leaving were driving along King William Road. Clayton wanted to vomit, because of the effects of the smoke, and they turned into Victoria Drive to enable him to go to the toilet for that purpose.

Coroner's Inquest

Each of the two officers I have mentioned and also Constable Hudson were shown individually to Mr James and to Mr Williamson, in the presence of the Inspectors. Mr James said then, and repeated in evidence at the inquest, that he had never seen any of these officers before. Mr Williamson was equally positive that they were not the men whom he had seen run into Kintore Avenue.

At this inquest Constables Clayton, Cawley and Hudson each declined on legal advice to answers questions on the grounds that their answers might tend to incriminate them. They were legally entitled to this privilege.

At this inquest there was no evidence that during the evening of the 10th May any of the three officers was nearer than about 300 yards [275 m] from the place where Dr Duncan was thrown into the river, and there is no evidence that any person other than Mr James and Mr Williamson was in the vicinity at the relevant times.

I find that the deceased was George Ian Ogilvie Duncan,
>Aged 41 years,
>Doctor of Philosophy,

and lecturer of Law at the University of Adelaide,
>late of 'Lincoln House',
>45 Brougham Place,
>North Adelaide.

He died shortly after 11.00 pm on the 10th May, 1972 in the River Torrens, Adelaide.

The cause of his death was drowning due to violence on the part of persons of whose identity there is no evidence.

The Death of Dr Duncan

The coroner had made one error. James had not crawled after the attackers; he moved away from them. But it did seem unusual, given the time it would have taken James to follow this route with a broken ankle, that the attackers had not fled before James sighted them again.

> At this inquest Constables CLAYTON, CAWLEY and HUDSON each declined on legal advice to answer questions on the ground that their answers might tend to incriminate them. They were legally entitled to this privilege.
>
> At this inquest there was no evidence that during the evening of the 10th May any of the three officers was nearer than about 300 yards from the place where Dr. DUNCAN was thrown into the river, and there is no evidence that any person other than Mr. JAMES and Mr. WILLIAMSON was in the vicinity at the relevant times.
>
> I find that the deceased was George Ian Ogilvie
> DUNCAN,
> Aged 41 years,
> Doctor of Philosophy,
> and lecturer of Law at the University of Adelaide,
> late of 'Lincoln
> House',
> 45 Brougham Place,
> NORTH ADELAIDE.
>
> He died shortly after 11.00 p.m. on the 10th May, 1972 in the River Torrens, Adelaide.
>
> The cause of his death was drowning due to violence on the part of persons of whose identity there is no evidence.

Inquest conclusion

Coroner's Inquest

The *News* beat the *Advertiser* to the story, trumpeting the inquest's findings on its front page: 'VIOLENCE IN DUNCAN DEATH: But finding open'. It seemed incredible on one level but also patently obvious on the other: no one had been able definitively to identify the attackers, and especially at the point of the assault. Roger James refused to be interviewed when approached by journalists in Sydney. 'He said it is all over now and he doesn't want to say anything,' said his partner, Tony Monopoli. Hudson also declined to comment to the press; Cawley and Clayton could not be located.

Horst Lücke realised that Duncan had not only been labelled a homosexual – based on the shape of his anus – but had been killed in a gay bashing. He made a personal statement to the *Advertiser* that there was no evidence Duncan had committed any offence on the night of 10 May, and 'whether he had been a homosexual or not, he had been a courteous and likeable colleague'. He added: 'He was a gentle, scholarly man who was utterly devoted to scholarship.' The following day the Attorney-General confirmed that the government would offer a $5000 reward for information leading to a conviction in the case. The reward would later be increased but no sum would ever be paid out.

Before the adjournment of the inquest Rod Matheson had commented: 'I have not the slightest doubt the police officers who were appointed to investigate this matter have investigated it thoroughly and that their investigations are continuing.' Cleland replied: 'I agree. No one could have done more.'

The Duncan case was officially at a stalemate. In just over three weeks New Scotland Yard would be called in.

CHAPTER 6

New Scotland Yard Report

John McKinna had been a brigadier in the Australian Army, serving from 1937 and including World War II. His distinguished service had earned him the Companion of the Order of St Michael and St George, with later appointment as Commander of the British Empire. He became Police Commissioner of South Australia in 1957 and was due to retire the month after Duncan's death upon reaching the age of 65. He and Premier Don Dunstan had had numerous disagreements and were hostile to each other. But McKinna had moved quickly in the Duncan case, appointing two independent Criminal Investigation Bureau inspectors on 12 May – two days after the killing – when Constable Harris, on duty at the Torrens police station that night, reported seeing Cawley in the vicinity.

During June 1972, however, evidence at the inquest increasingly was painting the police in a poor light, especially with the *Advertiser*'s in-depth reporting of the various testimonies. McKinna was not particularly adept at managing public relations with the media, and Dunstan was convinced that no one else within police ranks would be a suitable replacement. As early as October 1970, while in London, he had initiated a recruitment process through South Australia's Agent-General. Harold Salisbury was chosen after another candidate withdrew at the last minute from contract negotiations. It would be a decision that Dunstan would come to regret. In 1978 he sacked Salisbury for withholding information that police maintained secret files, including on homosexuals or 'sex deviates'. A royal commission later found that Salisbury indeed had misled the government.

McKinna was not informed of Dunstan's appointment, later claiming he had 'trained a number of senior local men who could have done the job well'. He briefed Salisbury at a handover in late June. The new commissioner was pictured in the press attending the coroner's findings in the Duncan case. Soon after Attorney-General Len King made the offer of a free pardon to anyone who could help police with their enquiries.

On 13 July Cawley and Clayton joined Hudson and tendered their resignations from SA Police. When Dunstan met with Salisbury, he expressed his government's disquiet over the affair: 'I said to him on his appointment that I was not happy with the way in which police had conducted the investigation, and I believed that that should be checked.' Salisbury's response was to look to his home country and recommend seeking the services of the murder squad of the London Metropolitan Police. After consulting with its commissioner, it was agreed to send two detectives from New Scotland Yard. Salisbury briefed the police union which indicated it would support his decision:

> The association never at any time would consider being a party to any action that may attempt to cover up any wrongdoing by its members. But, on the other hand, we would point out that until such time as it has been shown that some person has committed a wrong, then it is his privilege, the same as anyone else, to be deemed innocent.

A police press conference was called for 27 July at 7.15 pm. But Salisbury was nowhere to be seen. Superintendent Noel Lenton, the head of the CIB, handed out a prepared statement and declined to answer questions. The statement was a blunt admission that drastic measures were necessary both to reinvigorate the investigation and rebuild community trust:

> The Duncan case is a matter of public concern.
>
> It is of even greater concern for the Police Force of SA, which feels that inevitably misconstruction, both natural and mischievous, must develop in the particular, though difficult and nebulous, circumstances of the case.
>
> It is known that many ideas are being bandied about that would not stand up in the face of the already established facts.
>
> It is also known that there is some public uneasiness over the situation where the force itself is investigating a case of alleged crime where certain doubts have been expressed

The Death of Dr Duncan

directly and by innuendo on its own role in this business.

Although everything possible has been done, and is being done, in the investigation it is felt that, to show that absolute impartiality is being exercised, an outside and detached investigation will dispel any question of bias or favour.

The New Scotland Yard officers arrived in Australia on 5 August. They were Detective Chief Superintendent Robert (Bob) McGowan and Detective Sergeant Charles O'Hanlon. McGowan was 50, 'short and rugged' with a pronounced Scottish brogue, according to the *Sunday Mail*, but also 'with a face that looks as if it might have stopped a few fists during his 26 years in the Police Force'. His colleague, O'Hanlon, aged 35, meanwhile was described as 'tall, dark, and could be called handsome' and a 'dapper dresser'.

Arrival of the New Scotland Yard detectives

New Scotland Yard Report

McGowan boasted that he had led 22 murder investigations and solved 21, and had the name and fingerprints for the last. 'I have not come all this way to be a failure,' he said, words he would later rue. He refuted suggestions he was in Adelaide to investigate SA Police: 'I am not here to investigate a police force. I am here to investigate a death.' He refused even to describe Duncan's killing as a murder. He and O'Hanlon joined the Adelaide CIB detectives – a nine-man team – in a command post on the sixth floor of police headquarters in Angas Street. He instituted his own card index and filing systems, similar to those he had used at the Yard, and with O'Hanlon started ploughing through a mass of documents.

Within three weeks a call was made for public assistance in the case. A couple who had approached Roger James on Victoria Drive seeking directions was asked to come forward. A man who was seen on the banks of the Torrens that night holding a book was also sought. None of these people, however, would be identified in the final New Scotland Yard report. As noted, there was an even more intriguing request from O'Hanlon: 'Enquiries had revealed that before his death Dr Duncan had on at least four occasions had [sic] dined with different men aged about 30 at an Unley restaurant.' This suggested that Duncan may have been active on the dating scene with younger men, all of it happening within a brief seven-week period. But, again, there was no reference in the report.

The team that produced the report would ultimately interview 395 people, including those who had already appeared before the inquest. Roger James, while he was battling press allegations of withholding evidence, said: 'Despite all this unpleasantness, I have been treated with great courtesy by the men from Scotland Yard.' James changed his tune after the report, which was critical of him, was released. In 2005 he called McGowan and O'Hanlon 'a couple of dodos' and said: 'They were a waste of time ... they were rude, incompetent, they were just here to have a good time.' Mick O'Shea, who later made claims of a police cover-up in the Duncan case, was asked to write a statement for the report when he expected a full interview. He said that one of the Yard detectives had told him 'that there was nothing you could do when policemen closed ranks. He said it was the hardest type of investigation.' But O'Shea added: 'The consensus among the blokes in the force was that they were just a couple of old warbs from London.'

O'Hanlon's interviewing tactics were brought to the fore with a later statement in court from one of the unnamed witnesses. He described the detective as 'rude' and 'vulgar', claiming he had played with a sex toy – a vibrator – during the interview while asking: 'What would you do with this?' O'Hanlon would later demonstrate that he had form in such matters. After returning to Britain he was sentenced in 1976

New Scotland Yard Report

to seven years' jail for his role in a pornography protection racket. Meanwhile, McGowan had been sentenced in 1974 to three years' jail for evading value-added tax as a company director. They may have been crimes unrelated to murder, but it was still corrupt conduct. It could hardly be seen as inspiring confidence in the work of McGowan and O'Hanlon, or of New Scotland Yard.

The report was dated 2 October 1972 and consisted of 131 paragraphs. On 24 October, 80 days after the Yard's arrival, Commissioner Salisbury called a press conference at police headquarters. He was joined by McGowan, O'Hanlon and Deputy Commissioner Laurence Draper on the podium. All were stony-faced. Salisbury issued a press release, prefaced by the words: 'What I propose to do is read you a statement, and after that there will be no questions and no answers.' Salisbury had avoided the spotlight at the beginning of the Yard investigation, and was doing so again at its conclusion:

> As was said at the time when the Government was asked to call in the New Scotland Yard detectives, an entirely independent investigation by an outside force was the only way in which the Duncan case could be satisfactorily brought to a conclusion. That investigation has been carried out meticulously, in the greatest possible detail, and on the evidence submitted to the Crown Solicitor the decision has been made that there are inadequate grounds for a prosecution.

Don Dunstan tried to make the best of bad news by saying: 'I think the result shows that the SA Police Force did make a meticulous investigation.' Salisbury, however, having recommended to the premier to call in the Yard, must have been deeply embarrassed that no charges would be laid. But for a case that had attracted such public attention and concern – particularly over allegations of police involvement – to refuse to answer press questions was self-defeating. The *Advertiser* reported that it was 'understood' that the investigation had turned up nothing already known by Inspectors Lehmann and Turner. South Australian detectives were quoted as saying 'the decision to hold an inquest before all avenues of the police enquiry had been exhausted had hamstrung the investigation'. This was one conclusion of the Yard report, given that a witness had lied at the inquest such that their testimony would now potentially be tainted if the matter proceeded to trial.

Attorney-General Len King, who had ordered the inquest, addressed the House of Assembly and confirmed he had read the report. The decision that there was insufficient evidence had been made by the Crown Solicitor but also confirmed by Rod Matheson, counsel assisting the coroner during the inquest. But it was leaked to the press that the report had recommended prosecutions be launched – against three men. It was also later revealed that Salisbury and the Yard detectives apparently had privately agreed that prosecutions would have

New Scotland Yard Report

C.1/7	**METROPOLITAN POLICE**

Central Officer's Special Report

CRIMINAL INVESTIGATION DEPARTMENT,
New Scotland Yard,

2nd day of October 1972

SUBJECT
Doctor George Ian Ogilvie DUNCAN - enquiries into his death.

TO: COMMISSIONER OF POLICE, ADELAIDE.

Reference to Papers

C.R. 222/1972/129

1. This report appertains to enquiries made into the death of Dr. George Ian Ogilvie DUNCAN, aged 41 years, (born 20th July, 1930), a Doctor of Philosophy and Lecturer in Law at Adelaide University who died as a result of drowning in the Torrens Lake shortly after 11 p.m. on Wednesday, 10th May, 1972.

2. The circumstances surrounding his death are shrouded in mystery and one can only be guided by the only eye witness to the occurrence, namely

Stat. Pp. 56-66
Depn. Pp. 5-46

Roger Wesley JAMES, aged 27 years unemployed, who at the time of the incident was resident at 2 Prospect Road, FITZROY, South Australia, but has since moved to an address in Sydney.

3. He portrays how both DUNCAN and himself were set upon by a number of men on the banks of the Torrens Lake and thrown into the water, during the process of which he broke his ankle. He vaguely describes the persons concerned and has since been unable to identify them and to date no person has been apprehended in connection with this matter.

4. Before continuing further, it would be as well to outline Dr. DUNCAN's background, the

New Scotland Yard report

occurred in England. However, there were other issues of concern in relation to homosexual men with no connection to the case who suddenly found themselves visited by police. As CAMP said: 'Trying to get more evidence ... the CIB has charged into private homes and into workplaces. People have lost their jobs and been thrown out of home as a result ... What price justice?'

This impact was only reported in the gay press, for the mainstream media focused on calls that immediately sprang up for the report to be made public. King declined as its release 'could damage reputations' – Dunstan said it would be 'grossly libellous' – and because no charges had been laid. In parliament the Deputy Leader of the Opposition, Robin Millhouse, called for a royal commission, followed by journalist Paul Foss, but they were swiftly rebuffed. Over the years, with the continued refusal of successive governments of both persuasions to publish, rumours developed that the report named people high-up in Adelaide society – including politicians.

In June 2002, 30 years after Duncan's death, Attorney-General Michael Atkinson announced in parliament that the New Scotland Yard report would finally be made public. He revealed that the report previously had been protected by the provisions of the later *Freedom of Information Act*, which were due to expire in October. The government had consulted with the Leader of the Opposition and the Shadow Attorney-General, as well as the people they were able to contact who were named in the report. Atkinson confirmed that the report contained no names of 'current or former Members of Parliament, the Judiciary, the media or the police force amongst them'. He advised that the names of witnesses who came forward under protection of immunity would be kept secret, but then:

> This brings me to the final group of people named in the Report – the innocent people who happened to be in the vicinity of the incident when it took place or who were indirectly involved in some other way. The Government has decided to release the names of these people (although it has deleted some addresses). This is despite objections from some of them who we were able to contact. We have taken the view that the only way to end speculation about the Report is to release as many names and as much content as possible. This view has not been reached lightly. The Government has had to face the difficult task of balancing the public interest in releasing the Report against the right of individuals to privacy.

Atkinson also made mention of Roger James:

> Mr James ... is named throughout the Report and has legitimate reasons for not wanting it to be released. For instance, the Report unfairly refers to Mr James as a suspected drug addict. Perhaps more offensively it suggests that Mr James did not co-operate with police or was hiding information.

James indeed had come under sustained criticism in the report. One blistering sentence revealed: 'In all, he is a most unsatisfactory witness who appears to treat the matter lightly, considering the importance of his evidence.' This was one reason the report condemned the holding of the inquest before police investigations had concluded as James 'would never afterwards alter what he said, being afraid of having charges preferred against him'. But as well, 'doubts would arise as to the credibility of anything he said'. A friend of James claimed he had been betrayed by the state government:

> It is fear of exactly this sort of situation that makes people reluctant to come forward as witnesses to hate crimes. The Attorney-General has over-ruled a Supreme Court judge who found there were good reasons for the suppression of Roger's name. It means that promises to protect the identity of witnesses are worthless.

Atkinson moved a motion that 'this House resolve to authorise the publication' of the report, which was passed. The following day the Duncan case exploded in the media, but the focus was not on James. The *Advertiser* ran a five-page story with the front-page headline: 'Duncan killing: Scotland Yard report released after 30 years and finds ... VICE POLICE WERE GUILTY'. Black-and-white photos of Cawley, Clayton and Hudson were set against a colour image looking south across the Torrens to the place of Duncan's and James' attack. The front page also quoted paragraph 124 of the report:

> What really points to their guilt is their actions afterwards. No Police officer would fail to give evidence at an inquest if he had nothing to hide, and we know that they even sacrificed their professional careers in order to maintain their silence.

The paragraph had concluded: 'Thinking as Police officers, they attempted to rescue Duncan and rather than tell lies on oath at the inquest, they preferred not to incriminate themselves.' But elsewhere was even more damning because McGowan – who had authored the report – declared that 'from information from witnesses and their subsequent actions at the inquest it would seem more than likely they were the persons who committed the offence'.

The report's publication was an unwelcome irony for Cawley, Clayton and Hudson. As will be revealed in the next chapter, Cawley and Clayton had been acquitted of Duncan's manslaughter in 1988 – 14 years earlier. There had been found to be insufficient evidence to bring Hudson to trial. Clayton claimed that the release of the report had 'dealt him an injustice': 'I've said from the very beginning that I wasn't involved; it's easy for them to put this report out now, but it isn't fair ... I have been through the judicial system.' Cawley declined to comment while Hudson could not be contacted.

The sole focus on Cawley, Clayton and Hudson points to a crucial contradiction at the heart of the New Scotland Yard report. For it confirmed the findings of the inquest that the attack on Duncan and James was by men 'who were four in number'. The report thus had failed at the first hurdle: the mystery fourth man remained precisely that – a mystery. This squared with Mick O'Shea's later claim that the Yard detectives had said identification was unachievable given police had closed ranks.

The report also failed to provide a timeline so that the bustling activities of everyone on the riverbank that night could be accounted for. For example, it quoted one of the unnamed witnesses that Mr X – who was thrown in before Duncan and James – arrived at around 10.20 pm, and Mr X himself that he was thrown into the water 'somewhere in the region of 10.30 pm'. Yet the report said that Cawley and Clayton left the hotel about 10.30 pm, meaning they first had to drive across town to the toilet block and park. Clayton then went to the toilet – ostensibly to vomit – while Cawley told two uniformed policemen parked in a car to clear off. The report said this was at about 10.40 pm, but the inquest had it potentially 10 minutes earlier. But five minutes after 10.40 pm, Williamson was making his way to sit on the bench, making it highly likely he would have witnessed the attack on Mr X.

This timing also took no account of the attack on Osborne

which, according to the inquest, occurred in the toilet just before 10.30 pm. Osborne was not even mentioned in the report.

However, the report's main attention was on Cawley, Clayton and Hudson, but especially Cawley and Clayton and their claim that they had been at the riverbank for 10 minutes between 10.30 and 10.40 pm, when the main attack occurred around 11 pm. McGowan worked methodically to unpick their evidence, particularly on the basis of their initial interviews with Inspectors Lehmann and Turner:

> If we examine what they say, it is fairly obvious that their statements were made without much thought and were far from the actual truth but an excuse for their presence off duty at the Torrens Lake on the evening of 10th May, 1972.
>
> Both Cawley and Clayton say they attended the function for Constable Mildenhall, leaving at approximately 10.30 pm which is borne out by another witness. Their intention was to visit an address in North Adelaide and afterwards go to an hotel at Findon.
>
> Cawley drove his car with Clayton as passenger and as they went near the City Bridge, Clayton felt sick and it was decided that they should therefore stop at the gents toilet in Victoria Drive.
>
> On arrival in Victoria Drive, Cawley parked his car opposite the toilets and Clayton got out of the car and made his way to the gents toilet. Cawley states that prior to Clayton

leaving the car, he, Cawley, had spotted another car a short distance in front containing two men whom he though might be there for the purpose of robbing homosexuals. He mentioned this to Clayton.

He then went to a Police car on the opposite side of the road and spoke to Police Constables Smedley and Maynard, saying, 'Would you mind leaving the area for ten minutes or so, you're buggering up our poofters.' ... This was indeed a peculiar statement to make to the officers if he was keeping observation not on homosexuals but on persons who were likely to rob homosexuals.

Having got rid of the Police car containing the two officers, he apparently then loses interest in the car containing the two men and makes his way to the toilet to see Clayton.

Having met up with Clayton, he then gives a fantastic account of how he saw Constable Harris looking in some bushes and thinking he might be investigating something, says words to the effect, 'Do you want us to fuck off?'

Of course, the version supplied by Constable Harris is totally different. He says that he was patrolling along the City Bridge when he was hailed by Mr Fitzgerald who has a shop near the banks of the River Torrens. He started walking back in that direction and as he walked down the steps by the City Bridge he was confronted by Cawley and he said to him, 'Good-day, John.' Cawley's surprising reply was, 'Fuck off, fuck off.'

Harris noticed there was another man in his company but could not discern his features. In any event he knew Cawley as a member of the Vice Squad and formed the opinion that he was keeping observation on homosexuals. He joined Fitzgerald and they went to his premises for coffee.

Cawley and Clayton would have us believe that they spent a mere ten minutes at the Torrens and afterwards decided against keeping their previous appointments and returned to Carrington Street where Clayton's car was parked and both then went home. Apart from a preliminary interest in a car containing two men which had disappeared when they returned to their car, they had not interested themselves in other matters that night.

Unfortunately, this is far from the truth. First of all we have Cawley speaking to three Police officers, clearing them from the scene, with the inference that he was on duty and dealing with homosexuals.

Then the men whom Cawley refers to as being in the car whom he suspected of waiting to rob homosexuals were obviously [Witnesses D and B] who did not move from the scene until almost midnight that night and who were themselves homosexuals. In fact, [Witness D] later identified Cawley as one of the men seen by him running on the lawns near the toilets. He also identified Hudson as being one of the persons he saw leaning against a parking meter.

I am also bearing in mind that Cawley and Clayton say they went to the Torrens about 10.40 pm and were there for about ten minutes, but shortly before 11 pm Cawley is telling Harris, 'Fuck off' indicating that he is working.

Then there is the evidence of Williamson, if we are going

to accept that he is now telling the truth, saying that Clayton and Hudson were threatening him near the area where Duncan was drowned about 11 pm.

I think the most damaging part of Clayton's statement is that having spent about ten minutes at the Torrens, Cawley drove him to the car park in Carrington Street where he entered his car and drove home.

If we really believed him, we would accept that the time then would be approximately 11 pm but, of course, this is shown to be false by Constables Howie and O'Shea who see him in Carrington Street at 11.50 pm, making his way home. Clayton would find it extremely difficult to explain away his activities during this time.

Is not the truth of the matter that Hudson, Cawley and Clayton and possibly one other officer, having had a number of drinks at the function, decided to go to the Torrens Lake and stir up the homosexuals who frequent there? Having arrived there, possibly Clayton did go to the toilet and saw [Mr X], who was afterwards thrown in the river because they accepted that he was a homosexual.

Afterwards, they spotted Dr Duncan and James together on the seat but had to ascertain that no witnesses were about and therefore made certain that Williamson left the area before throwing Duncan and James into the water.

This final paragraph references the fact that Kevin Williamson was sitting on a bench on the upper path and was warded off by two out of a group of four men. Yet it makes no sense. Williamson recorded that the four men ran past him heading west before two of them urged him to leave. However, were this the case they first would have run straight past the bench on which Duncan and James supposedly were sitting, who would have been alerted to danger or at the very least to strange goings-on. It was highly likely the men were heading to the toilet block for this was their *modus operandi*, which had worked so well with Mr X: to lure their victim from there to the water's edge for the attack. Duncan and James can only have arrived on the scene – separately or together – after Williamson had returned to his car.

The New Scotland Yard report was estimated to have cost the state government $13,000. No new key witnesses had been identified – in fact, no new evidence had been found – and Duncan's entry into the beat was still unknown. As it had not been within the report's ambit, there also was no attempt to investigate further the inference drawn from Cawley's statements to uniformed officers that South Australian Vice Squad officers engaged in terrorising homosexuals at the No. 1 Beat. A local joke in the poorest taste had emerged: that 'Duncan got a dunkin'' as part of the Vice Squad's 'teach Adelaide's poofters to swim' campaign. But the SA Police Association – the police union – was certain that there were no cases 'of police officers acting as "decoys" or *agents provocateurs*, to secure the conviction of homosexuals'. The *Advertiser* also editorialised that the detectives' efforts had:

dispelled the grounds for suspicion, whether it was originally justified or not, that the SA Police Force had not done all within its power to solve the case. They have made it clear that the effort to solve the case can now be relaxed, in confidence that everything possible has been done ... It is a tragedy to have to add that the case remains unsolved.

The Duncan case now lay in abeyance for nearly 13 years. When it next hit the headlines it was on the basis of claims that SA Police had engaged in a cover-up after all.

CHAPTER 7

Reopening of Case and Trial

On 10 May 1973, the first anniversary of Duncan's death, the *Advertiser* carried 32 notices in its 'In Memoriam' column. One read: 'In memory of George Duncan. He taught justice and died without it.' The night before, buildings around Adelaide had been daubed with slogans referring to the killing. Fences at Victoria Park Racecourse were emblazoned: 'Duncan was murdered one year ago by SA Police – remember'. The western wall of the new Holiday Inn in the city read: 'Duncan is dead – why?' At the first national conference of CAMP a week later, 10 May was adopted as an annual commemoration date. The Duncan case was becoming a rallying cause around the country.

There was another anniversary event organised by gay liberationists. Four effigies were hung from the University of Adelaide footbridge before being hastily removed by authorities. Each effigy bore an identifying placard: 'Cawley', 'Clayton', 'Hudson' or 'O'Shea'. Mick O'Shea was not generally associated with the Duncan case, at least in the public eye. He had been interviewed at length at the inquest – the only

The Death of Dr Duncan

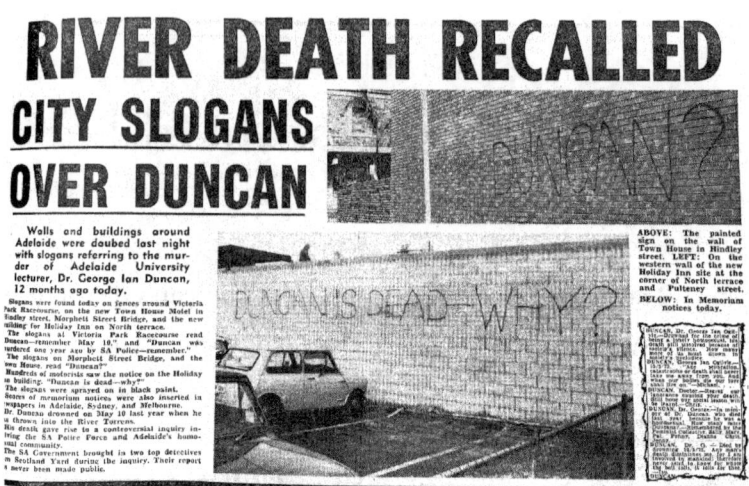

Newspaper coverage on the first anniversary of Duncan's death

Vice Squad officer other than the three who gained the most publicity – but his name notably did not appear in the coroner's final summary as he had an alibi that night. This was even after he had been identified by an anonymous witness as one of the people running around the boatsheds. Strangely, O'Shea had been driven out to the workplace of the witness and shown to him. It was another example of police not using proper line-ups for the purposes of identification, as earlier experienced by Roger James. It was also, O'Shea later claimed, part of a plan by police to discredit the witness when he came before the inquest.

Reopening of Case and Trial

The rumours about O'Shea had never gone away, especially among the local gay community, that he was the mystery fourth man who had been involved in the attack on Duncan and James.

O'Shea had followed in his father's footsteps, joining SA Police as a cadet aged 17 and completing three years of training. At the time of the inquest he was 23 and had been a member of the Vice Squad for about 18 months. He was targeted from the very early days of the case. Paul Foss in his provocative August 1972 piece in *National U* had commented that after the inquest: 'I was dismayed that the Vice Squad members implicated in the case, Constables Clayton, Cawley, Hudson and O'Shea, could so easily maintain a conspiracy of silence.' Foss had posed a series of questions of O'Shea:

> Why has he lost two stone of weight, cut his hair and changed his place of residence since May 10th?
>
> Why was he in Royal Adelaide Hospital at the end of May and seen walking around on crutches? Did he sustain an injury on the night of Duncan's murder?
>
> How could he drink for five and a half hours at the King's Head Hotel party when it is known that he had recently suffered from hepatitis?
>
> Why did O'Shea tell his friends and family that he was going to spend the night of May 10th at a Greek restaurant in Hindley St when in fact he attended the party at King's Head Hotel?

Why did O'Shea state that he had only been in the vicinity of the Torrens bog three or four times in the last three months? It is known that O'Shea tried to solicit Mr P [whom Foss interviewed] outside the Torrens bog early last year.

If O'Shea's description appeared often during testimony of the witnesses, why was O'Shea's alibi not corroborated by calling Mildenhall and others who attended the party?

Is it true that pressure is being put upon the premier Mr Dunstan to slow down the investigation of Duncan's murder by the CIB? O'Shea's father, also in the police force, is past president of the Norwood branch of the ALP – that jewel in Dunstan's eye – and present executive member. A scandal at this time is not exactly desired before elections.

The final question – with allegations involving Dunstan – was explosive. But *National U* was a small interstate student publication and only several thousand copies made their way into South Australia. Stewart Cockburn of the *Advertiser* conducted his own investigations and declared that much of the material was 'based on unsubstantiated statements by un-named informants, on inaccurately researched facts from which unwarranted deductions are drawn'. O'Shea himself had no voice except for his union which indicated it was considering suing on his behalf. This never occurred. In 1981 O'Shea was invalided out of the police force on a disability pension, before later suffering a nervous breakdown.

Reopening of Case and Trial

O'Shea became collateral damage in the Duncan case. Yet it is a simple fact that at the inquest he had never been subjected to the police grilling of the other three Vice Squad officers, had not been suspended nor had resigned from the police force. The New Scotland Yard report also did not refer to him. His one mistake was to be at Mildenhall's farewell party when he was on duty; he was later demoted back to uniformed work. It made him bitter for he claimed he had been directed by his supervising sergeant to attend the event.

On 30 July 1985, more than 13 years after the drowning, O'Shea found his voice. In a series of articles in the *Advertiser* by Mike McEwen – an exclusive for which he won a Walkley Award for excellence in journalism – O'Shea blew the Duncan case wide open. In the process he suffered the fate of many whistleblowers: accused of being a liar, a conspiracy theorist, a malcontent. He himself pointed the finger at McEwen for sensationalising the story. He 'quite clearly dudded me, used me up and spat me out,' O'Shea later said.

McEwen laid out O'Shea's main claims in six bullet points:

- *Forensic evidence, which could have implicated certain members of the police force in Dr Duncan's death, was never sought by investigating officers.*
- *A 'fourth man' widely thought by other policemen to have been in the company of three vice squad officers identified*

as being on the Torrens on the night of May 10, 1972, was never interviewed by investigating officers. Nor was he sought out by senior officers from Scotland Yard when they conducted an enquiry into the case after the inquest had failed to identify Dr Duncan's assailants.

- *It had been 'standard procedure' for certain members of the vice squad to 'terrorise' homosexuals on the banks of the River Torrens by throwing them into the water. At the Duncan inquest this had been specifically denied by members of the vice squad.*
- *On the night of May 10, 1972, at a send-off party in the city for a retiring member of the vice squad, there had been specific talk by certain members of the squad of 'going down to the river later to flick poofters in'.*
- *Evidence at the inquest was suppressed because of 'clear directions' by senior police officers that the truth, particularly in relation to vice squad policing routines, was not to be told.*
- *The general level of corruption in the vice squad at the time was such that there was mistrust and open malevolence between senior officers and junior ranks, and between individual members.*

In relation to the latter point O'Shea also declared that there had been 'a high level of animosity' between members of the Vice

Reopening of Case and Trial

Squad, Criminal Investigation Branch and uniformed officers, which had created 'personal feuds and vendettas'. This led to the most incendiary claim: 'In this atmosphere of "incompetence, deliberate fudging and mistrust" there had been a conspiracy of silence to protect certain members of the police force thought to have been involved in Duncan's drowning.'

O'Shea said he was mainly coming forward to clear his name as the alleged 'fourth man'. He knew who that person was, and it wasn't a police officer. He claimed it was a friend of Constable Mildenhall's who had attended the police farewell party on the night in question. The man was 'some sort of organiser' at a western suburbs hotel disco frequented by 'certain members of the Vice Squad'. The *Advertiser* interviewed two other former Vice Squad officers who corroborated O'Shea's story, but its attempts to trace the man had been fruitless.

It was also reported that Paul Turner, one of the two inspectors who led the early police investigation, agreed the fourth man 'had been pursued, but was never located'. He added:

> We were seriously hampered because people under investigation refused to answer any questions. People were reluctant, to be frank. Members of the vice squad and others who might have been associated with them had the attitude that they didn't want to be in it. For anyone to have come forward and said 'the fourth person was so and so' they would have had to say who the other three were.

But Turner otherwise rejected O'Shea's claims, which obviously cast doubt over the investigation led by Lehmann and himself.

Former South Australian premier, Don Dunstan, who was now head of the Victorian Tourism Commission, claimed that he had always suspected a police cover-up. But he also said that the still unreleased New Scotland Yard report had not produced enough evidence for a case to be mounted, although 'there were many pointers'. The *Advertiser* also contacted Roger James. It was believed that because he had been unable to identify the three men who threw Duncan into the water, the fourth man who initially approached him – and of whom he had offered a good description – potentially was still out there. But James refused to be interviewed. 'It's flogging a dead horse,' he said. 'I'm not interested. I've done my lot.'

Brian Hudson was also located by Mike McEwen at his crash repair shop in Perth. He agreed with O'Shea's characterisation of the Vice Squad in 1972 as corrupt, saying many officers were 'on the take'. He confirmed as well that Vice Squad officers were throwing homosexuals into the Torrens, but denied being involved. He admitted that he had been the 'doorman' for the Mildenhall farewell party and that there were 'about 25 plainclothes police officers' at the party who should have been on duty. He had destroyed a list of the names – 'and there were plenty of people anxious to get hold of that, I can tell you,' he said. Finally, he claimed to have a letter 'from a source he would not name, which he says throws a completely new light on the mystery surrounding the case'. It would be his 'trump card' were he ever dragged back into the affair.

Two days after O'Shea's allegations, Labor Attorney-General Chris Sumner and the Police Commissioner announced that a special taskforce had been established to gather new evidence. The same week, and in advance of an upcoming state election, the Liberals announced that if elected they would establish a royal commission into the Duncan case:

> Some eminent lawyer from outside SA with no political affiliations or association with any political party should be appointed to conduct a totally independent enquiry, producing a report which can be made public to reassure South Australians. Allegations of political interference with the investigative process must always be matters of the gravest public concern and must be investigated regardless of when they are alleged to have occurred.

Sumner responded that the call was premature and irresponsible, with the potential 'to scare off people'. A week later he announced a $25,000 reward 'for the person first giving information leading to the arrest of the principal offender or offenders'. He also revealed that there would be immunity from prosecution for those giving evidence, and that the New Scotland Yard report, while not being released publicly, would be provided to the relevant spokespeople in the Opposition and the Democrats. He added that recent allegations of a political cover-up by *Advertiser* journalist Robert Ball were being investigated by the taskforce and he would welcome the newspaper's cooperation.

The election in December saw the return of the Labor Party and the royal commission never eventuated. The police taskforce completed its interim report on 10 January 1986 after a six-month investigation, and forwarded it to the Crown Prosecutor, Paul Rice. On 5 February the Duncan case took a dramatic turn. Three arrests were made in two states on charges of manslaughter, with anything tending to identify the three individuals initially suppressed. Those arrested were eventually named as the three former Vice Squad officers linked to the Duncan case:

- Francis John Cawley, 37, labourer
- Michael Kenneth Clayton, 38, hotelier
- Brian Edwin Hudson, 51, company director.

Cawley appeared in the Para Districts Magistrates Court and was remanded to the Adelaide Magistrates Court on a $2000 surety. Clayton appeared in the Kadina Court of Summary Jurisdiction before two justices of the peace. He was remanded on his own recognisance of $1000 and a surety of $1000, and was also ordered to reside at his own home. Hudson was living in Western Australia and appeared in the

Reopening of Case and Trial

Perth Magistrates Court where he was granted $2000 bail, with a $2000 surety, on condition he report daily to police. An extradition application was granted and Hudson was ordered to appear in the Adelaide Magistrates Court at a later date. All three also had to surrender their passports.

The arrests were announced by Chris Sumner who was joined by Rice when the media were briefed. Sumner said the taskforce's investigation 'had revealed evidence additional to that obtained in 1972'. He added the taskforce had found no evidence that the original investigation 'had been thwarted due to political or senior police intervention to cover up'. One of O'Shea's major claims in relation to police interference therefore had already been rejected, and the *Advertiser*'s editor was also forced to admit that its source concerning political interference had been 'reliable' rather than 'impeccable'.

On 3 March 1986 Cawley, Clayton and Hudson appeared in Court 29 in the Adelaide Magistrates Court. They were formally arraigned for a preliminary hearing, which would commence on 8 September. This procedure in place in South Australia meant that the prosecution would present its case which, if it were determined that a *prima facie* case had been made against one or more of the defendants, would result in committal for trial. Cawley, Clayton and Hudson thus would only be sent to trial if the prosecution could convince a magistrate that enough evidence existed to do so. At trial, both the defence and the prosecution would then present their individual cases for judgement.

At the conclusion of the arraignment Hudson was heard talking in the court by an *Advertiser* journalist. 'No one's interested now,' Hudson said. 'They couldn't care less. But they will. This will be bigger than the Chamberlains.' He almost seemed to be boasting, yet the case of Azaria Chamberlain was now one of national infamy since first hitting the headlines in 1980. What kind of development in the Duncan case could possibly top that, and did it relate to the mystery letter?

At the start of the preliminary hearing none of the accused entered a plea. When Rice opened the prosecution case before the Chief Magistrate, Nick Manos, he told the court that an unknown fourth man was also involved with the accused men in the death of Duncan. But he also made the intriguing admission that 'the prosecution doesn't discount the possibility there were other people'. He then called his first witness to the stand: Mick O'Shea. O'Shea was in a difficult position, for in his claims he was having to acknowledge that his evidence had been untruthful at the coronial inquest. In effect, he had committed an offence but, worse, he had done so while a serving police officer. Clayton's counsel, Michael Abbott QC, cross-examined O'Shea and secured an admission he had lied under oath. The chief magistrate twice warned O'Shea about possible self-incrimination but he said he wanted to continue giving evidence. In explaining his allegations of a police cover-up, O'Shea claimed that two inspectors had persuaded him to agree to be identified by one of the unnamed witnesses; this was intended to discredit the witness at the inquest as it was known O'Shea was still at the farewell party when Duncan drowned. O'Shea in court also denounced the *Advertiser* coverage, which had led him to take legal action against the newspaper. He did not after all know the identity of the unknown fourth man and denied he had said several police had committed perjury during the inquest.

Over several weeks Rice presented his case to the court. Even with the new evidence from O'Shea, however, the Duncan killing still essentially revolved around James as the sole witness with no knowledge as to how and when Duncan had entered the beat. Then the police statement of Bobby Callaghan was introduced which challenged James' version of events. As noted, Callaghan had claimed that Duncan and James were walking together before being attacked from behind by three out of four men who ran over a wall to the lower path – with James being thrown in before Duncan. On this basis James may not have seen the attackers. Michael Abbott claimed this was consistent with James' inquest evidence that he had heard a group of voices 'above and behind' him. James now stated that he could not recall why he had said this; that he had first noticed the group of men approaching on the lower path. Abbott would claim in his summing up that James' evidence was 'not cogent or competent' and that he and O'Shea were candidates 'for the trophy for the worst witnesses of the year'.

Magistrate Manos sought access to the still unreleased New Scotland Yard report, but SA Police refused his request. On 29 October Manos brought down the first of two findings. He dismissed the charge against Hudson and ordered that he be discharged. This was not surprising on one level given that even Crown Prosecutor Rice had admitted that the evidence against Hudson was weaker than that against Cawley or Clayton. Hudson walked free from the court but refused to answer questions from the waiting media. The infamous letter that supposedly would clear him thus has never seen the light of day, and the notoriety of the Duncan case has not rivalled the Chamberlain case. He remains the only one of the three former Vice Squad officers linked to the Duncan affair who has never been tried in court.

Exactly three weeks later, Manos brought down his second finding: there was sufficient evidence to bring Cawley and Clayton to trial. He dismissed defence submissions that the court process after 14 years 'was an abuse of process of the court'. But nine days later Manos adjourned the case after Michael Abbott said he would seek a Supreme Court order to stop the trial for precisely this reason. This application was

Reopening of Case and Trial

heard in September 1987 before Justice Maurice O'Loughlin, who ultimately ruled that the trial should proceed.

On 13 September 1988 Cawley and Clayton pleaded not guilty in the Supreme Court to charges 'of having unlawfully killed Dr Duncan'. The trial was presided over by the same Justice O'Loughlin and ran until the 30th. As with the preliminary hearing neither Cawley nor Clayton testified in their defence. Justice O'Loughlin spent nearly four hours summing up to the jury of nine men and three women. He said the prosecution had argued that the weight of circumstantial evidence was sufficient to convict Cawley and Clayton, and that both had lied in their original interviews with police, demonstrating 'a conscience of guilt'. The defence's key argument was that no witnesses had identified either man as having attacked Duncan, and that O'Shea's evidence should be rejected or at least viewed as unreliable.

The jury retired mid-afternoon to consider its verdict. By that night they had failed to reach a verdict and were taken to a city hotel. Justice O'Loughlin advised that a majority verdict would be accepted, with 10 or 11 jurors in agreement, instead of a unanimous one. The following day at 11.05 am Cawley and Clayton were acquitted, Clayton unanimously and Cawley by majority. Their lawyer said the two were unlikely to seek compensation from the state government; they were 'just relieved' that the case had ended. The SA

Police Association added that its members would be 'pleased with the result which has dispelled any lingering doubt about the veracity of SA police. Police do not hold themselves above the law'.

There would be one last development in the Duncan case. On 3 April 1990 Chris Sumner tabled in the South Australian Parliament the 'Duncan Task Force Final Report' produced by the Internal Investigation Branch of SA Police. The task force had been commissioned on 1 August 1985 in response to the claims of Mick O'Shea, so its work had taken about 4½ years. Its initial brief was to:

- *identify the person or persons responsible for the death of Dr Duncan;*
- *determine Vice Squad police practices relative to homosexuals in 1972;*
- *revealing* [sic] *any allegations of corrupt practices amongst 1972 Vice Squad members;*
- *determine whether any of the 1972 enquiries were thwarted due to political interference.*

The task force's preliminary report had led to the charging of Cawley, Clayton and Hudson. But following the court hearings 'a number of questions relative to Vice Squad practices again surfaced', and the task force extended its work and timeline.

In relation to the second bullet point the report concluded:

> There is some suspicion that this practice may have occurred, however the absence of specifics and allegations from victims would tend to indicate it was not a common occurrence, and perhaps was, at the most, an isolated incident which has grown with the telling.
>
> Had it been common practice, then I would have expected victims to have come forward and raised this issue with the media or police, particularly in view of the wide and comprehensive media coverage at the time. It surely would have been common knowledge amongst homosexuals frequenting the Torrens 'beat' at that time.

This response was disingenuous. Male homosexual acts in 1972 were criminalised around the nation, helping to create a social climate of homophobia. The terrorisation of homosexuals by their bashing on beats by Vice Squad officers operated on dual levels. It damaged the victims physically and emotionally, but also dissuaded them from coming forward, given that such corrupt activity potentially would also manifest itself at a police station were a report to be made. As well, the victim possibly would have to admit to engaging in criminal behaviour as part of making the complaint. The idea of taking the matter to the media was also absurd given how many homosexual men were being forced to live closeted

The Death of Dr Duncan

DUNCAN TASK FORCE

FINAL REPORT

Dr. DUNCAN G. I. O. - Death of
(Died 10 May 1972 - Drowning due to violence)

CONFIDENTIAL.

Prepared for: Commissioner of Police.

Prepared by: Commander R.G. LEAN
Detective Chief Inspector J.D. LITSTER
Chief Inspector J.R. CASARETTO

February 1990

Duncan Task Force Final Report

lives. As Mick O'Shea has stated: 'There was never ever a complaint when [homosexuals] were bashed or otherwise thrown in the river because they had far too much to hide themselves.'

The foreword of the report, however, contained an important admission:

> The Task Force was mindful that this enquiry was conducted in a different police administrative environment from that which existed in 1972. Without being overly critical of the administration of that time, the policies, procedures and managerial techniques that existed then, were not as stringent as is the case today. Public scrutiny and expectation, have seen a number of fundamental changes made to the philosophy and structure of policing practices ...

But there was little joy for anyone hoping to find some kind of resolution of the Duncan case. The report's first recommendation was: 'No further enquiries be conducted relative to ... identifying the person or persons responsible for Dr Duncan's death unless further new evidence is forthcoming.' And so the situation has remained for over 30 years. The only major change occurred in 2021 when Crime Stoppers SA announced an increase in the government reward to $200,000.

In a 1993 ABC *7.30 Report* story Don Dunstan said:

The Death of Dr Duncan

The most we can hope for now is a *Crime and Punishment* scenario, where somebody with some guilty knowledge actually confesses. Because otherwise I don't see where we're to acquire additional evidence.

Dunstan was right. And so we wait.

PART III
GAY LAW REFORM

CHAPTER 8

1972 Decriminalisation Bill

For almost a month from 7 June the reporting of the Duncan inquest dominated Adelaide's media. It was difficult to pick up the *Advertiser* without seeing the story on the front page, together with swathes of verbatim reporting of the testimonies inside. Academics were held in high esteem in the community, and the senseless death of this recently arrived man – possibly at the hands of off-duty policemen – was shocking. But it was the revelation of Duncan's sexuality, which was front and centre on the first day of the inquest, that would concentrate and propel a wider debate. More than this: it marked the beginning of radical changes in South Australia's criminal law.

The colonists brought English law with them to Australia. It had never been codified against male homosexuality as such; its focus had always been on specific sexual behaviour. Buggery – anal sex – was first criminalised by Henry VIII in 1533, and in the beginning it was punishable by death. This code operated initially in every colony of Australia. It was not until 1859 – three years after the colony gained self-government – that the death penalty was removed in South Australia, although it had never been used. Over time the penalty was reduced from 10 years to life imprisonment, to a maximum of 10 years, though early on this included hard labour and even allowed for flogging. Key changes to South Australian law meant that, by 1935, attempting to procure or committing a male homosexual act whether in public or private was outlawed. These were the restrictions in place when Dr Duncan arrived.

The law operated in such a way to create a potent social taboo around male homosexuality (female homosexual acts were not criminalised). This could condemn such men to a life of fear and self-loathing. They could be disowned by their family, ostracised by their friends, sacked by their employer or evicted by their landlord. If brought before the courts they could be imprisoned or, worse, with their name published in the press, take their own lives. However, this did not prevent a burgeoning homosexual sub-culture from developing in South Australia from the 1930s, as like-minded men found ways of meeting in public and private. As noted, beats played an important role on both a social and sexual level, but various hotels around Adelaide became known meeting places and parties were held in private homes, although there was always the risk of being raided by police. Some men formed partnerships and moved in together but discretion was paramount, for homosexual sex – even in the privacy of one's bedroom – was a crime.

1972 Decriminalisation Bill

The punitive effects of the laws around male homosexual acts led to change in Britain. An infamous case involved the distinguished actor John Gielgud, who was knighted in June 1953 but four months later was arrested for 'importuning' an undercover police officer in a public toilet. Gielgud got off with a fine but later suffered a breakdown. The following year the brilliant mathematician and World War II codebreaker, Alan Turing, committed suicide after being subjected to court-mandated chemical castration. But the jailing of Lord Montagu of Beaulieu and others on homosexual charges prompted the government to commission what became the 1957 Wolfenden Report. This recommended decriminalisation of male homosexual acts, although the reform took another decade to be implemented.

These events had not gone unnoticed in South Australia. Indeed, Dr Duncan may well have been written out of gay history if Don Dunstan had had his way. In 1965, and soon after his appointment as Attorney-General, Dunstan secured Cabinet agreement to introduce a Bill to enact decriminalisation. While initially approved by the Labor Caucus, some members then withdrew their support. A nationwide survey two years later confirmed what they suspected: less than a quarter of respondents favoured liberalisation of the law. By 1970, however, the same pollsters found that over half now advocated the removal of criminal sanctions.

The Death of Dr Duncan

In December 1971, as Premier of South Australia, Don Dunstan announced an inquiry into the state's criminal law. It would be chaired by Justice Roma Mitchell, and homosexuality would come within its purview. Dunstan emphasised the need for the removal of:

> outmoded attempts of the criminal law to invade the spheres of private morality and social welfare. Our revision of the criminal law will leave people free to live their lives as they wish so long as they do not harm others.

The committee initially 'would tackle penal matters and then specific projects over a period of time'. But no precise timeframe was provided.

Homosexual men and women around Australia had already started to take matters into their own hands. In February 1971, the first meeting of the New South Wales branch of a lobby group called Campaign Against Moral Persecution (CAMP) had been held. The acronym was particularly apt as it was then the Australian vernacular for a homosexual man. Other branches of CAMP started to spring up, with South Australia's first meeting in September of that year.

CAMP SA members set up working groups to research and take action in the areas of law reform, psychology, public relations, and religious and moral issues. It was decided that law reform involving the decriminalisation of male homosexual acts 'was obviously going to be a long and difficult path', and it would be necessary to prepare a detailed submission to the Mitchell Committee. This was reported in February 1972 in the *Advertiser* with a CAMP member charging that the present laws allowed blackmail and violence to flourish and condoned employer discrimination against homosexuals.

The group also made a move into religious circles as the Church had substantial clout in the shaping of community attitudes and was often asked to comment on issues of sexual morality. The Anglican Bishop of Adelaide at first was strongly opposed, but later indicated he would not object to a relaxation of the laws: 'While I condemn the sin, I am extremely sorry for these unfortunate people. I don't think they should be put in prison.' The Catholic Archbishop correctly identified the confusion that existed in the dichotomy 'between illegal acts and immoral acts', although he reaffirmed the Church's view that deliberate homosexual acts were immoral. But Congregational and Methodist Church spokespeople expressed support for decriminalisation.

The Church position was taken as a sign to increase activity. CAMP started placing classified advertisements in Adelaide newspapers which read: 'CAMP assists homosexual people. Social, legal, political. Send SAE for latest newsletter and membership.' One anonymous correspondent replied: 'YOU FILTHY DIRTY ROTTEN PERVERTS[.] THE ANIMALS OF THE

The Death of Dr Duncan

FIELD HAVE HIGHER PRINCIPALS [sic] THAN "THINGS" LIKE YOU'. It was a brutal reminder there were people who would be stridently opposed to any relaxation of the laws relating to homosexuality.

But amid all the commotion about the Duncan case there had been an unexpected development. Two weeks after the inquest had commenced a group calling itself the Moral Freedom Committee wrote an open letter to South Australian parliamentarians urging decriminalisation. This group was mainly comprised of young heterosexual men and women who were members of the Humanist Society of South Australia. The letter stated:

> If one thing is clear from [the Duncan] incident – regardless of whether the parties were homosexuals – it is that certain persons prey on people they believe to be homosexuals and avoid prosecution because homosexuals will not come forward for fear of prosecution.
>
> The question of homosexual behaviour is a moral matter and therefore not the law's business. The law does not punish fornication and adultery; it should not punish homosexual behaviour.

This letter crossed paths with three *Advertiser* articles written by John Miles under the banner of 'The Homosexual Scene in Adelaide'. The first article, headlined 'Lively talkers, stylish dressers', hinted at Miles' approach to the subject:

1972 Decriminalisation Bill

It is as impossible to make accurate generalities about Adelaide homosexuals as it is about any other group of individuals, but they do have one thing in common – their sexual aberration. Otherwise, homosexuals in Adelaide range from whining, obvious queers to talented, charming, responsible men who live quietly, discreetly with other men.

Worse was to come for Miles revealed that homosexual men were of two main types: 'the "butch", who take the male role,

'The Homosexual Scene in Adelaide', Part 1

and the "bitch", who take the female role'. Miles also stated that 'many homosexuals among themselves adopt a patronising, sneering attitude to the "squares", the "peasantry", who are heterosexual'. It was a panoply of crass, verging on snide, stereotypes. A member of CAMP, David Hilliard, responded in a letter to the editor:

> Heavy stress is placed on bizarre and flamboyant aspects of the homosexual sub-culture, without a corresponding attempt to understand the need for human community and personal fulfilment behind this behaviour. But to expect a man whose first-hand knowledge is necessarily limited to write with any real insight on people whose sexual orientation he finds incomprehensible is perhaps to ask too much.

However, the *Advertiser* was about to take its first step in a campaign which would see it promote decriminalisation until its eventual success. On 1 July it issued an editorial headed 'Legalise Homosexuality'. The headline was semantically incorrect, but the message very clear:

> The present law on homosexuality cannot be justified. As the controversy stirred by the Duncan inquest suggests, it is one of the reasons why many homosexuals in Australia are forced to lead unhappy, sometimes tragic lives ... The State has no business in its citizens' bedrooms and the sooner it is completely removed from them, the better.

1972 Decriminalisation Bill

The Advertiser

Saturday, July 1, 1972

Legalise homosexuality

The present law on homosexuality cannot be justified. As the controversy stirred by the Duncan inquest suggests, it is one of the reasons why many homosexuals in Australia are forced to lead unhappy, sometimes tragic lives. As it stands, "any male person who, in public or private commits, or is party to the commission of . . . any act of gross indecency with another male person," is punishable by up to three years in gaol, although there is no similar charge for females.

The arguments in favor of retaining this law can be broken down into two basic positions. First, there is the argument that homosexuality is an immoral form of behaviour and therefore should be outlawed. But even if it could be easily determined which behaviour is immoral and which is not, it is still not the duty of the law to enforce a code of moral behaviour upon anyone. The law should only become involved when a certain mode of conduct is harmful to others which, in the case of homosexuality, it is not.

The second argument frequently used to support the existing law rests on the fear that many people who are not homosexuals would become so if the law were changed. But as the example of other countries has shown, there is no evidence that heterosexuals have any desire to become homosexuals just because they are no longer subject to punishment by the law. Of course, there should still be strong laws against corrupting the young, just as there are already strong heterosexual laws to protect the young.

Finally, it is sometimes argued that homosexuality should be outlawed because it is unnatural. Certainly, to most of the community it is, but that is no reason to punish or try to change those who practise it. Provided it is done in private between consenting adults, it is not offending or harming anyone, and that is where the matter should end. Thus it seems that the basis of the present law is, at best, unsound.

On the other hand, the argument in favor of legalising homosexual acts in private between consenting males is quite clear cut. Put simply, such acts harm no one and offend no one, and the law has no right to intervene in such a situation. To be fair, it should be stated that the law is not rigidly enforced by the police. However, it is objectionable that such a law exists at all. The State has no business in its citizens' bedrooms and the sooner it is completely removed from them, the better.

Advertiser editorial calling for gay law reform

The Death of Dr Duncan

Vol. 115, No. 35,469   30 Pages 7c

Homosexual Bill for S.A. Parlt.

By Political Reporter ERIC FRANKLIN

An LCP Member of the Legislative Council will introduce a Private Member's Bill to allow homosexual behaviour between consenting males in private in SA.

Mr. Hill . . . "it shouldn't be swept under the carpet."

STOP PRESS

Mr. Hill, MLC, said yesterday that he would move the Bill as soon as possible after Parliament began the session on July 18.

Mr. Hill said: "To my way of thinking the society will have to accept that some individuals cannot resist this sort of behaviour.

"They are a minority group and need some consideration from an enlightened and tolerant community.

"I like to think that in this State we have such a community."

Several young people, including psychologists, teachers and lawyers, had asked MPs to do something about homosexuality, he said.

Mr. Hill said he believed that radical social legislation of this kind should be put to Parliament by a private Member and not a political party.

He stressed that the Bill, now being drafted, would seek to protect the privacy only of those people who lived together.

The legislation certainly would not seek to put the seal of moral approval on homosexuality as such, nor would it condone this sort of behaviour.

Homosexual acts in public would remain unlawful on the grounds that they offended accepted standards of public decency.

Mr. Hill said he was not canvassing support from among his Parliamentary colleagues for the Bill.

He was moving the Bill because he thought recent publicity had caused people to think deeply about homosexuality.

"It is an issue which should not be swept under the carpet," Mr. Hill said.

Detectives

The nine-man special squad of detectives under Inspector C. E. Lehmann, set up yesterday to intensify police enquiries into the Duncan case, already has begun its task.

Members of the squad will re-examine all known clues and any new information gained.

The Chief of the CIB (Superintendent N. R. Lenton) said that any information given would be treated in the utmost confidence.

Detectives hope that a $5,000 reward and a free pardon offered yesterday by the Government might tempt somebody to give them the break they need.

● Govt. offer for Duncan case clues, P. 6.

Announcement of Murray Hill's Bill

1972 Decriminalisation Bill

LEGISLATIVE COUNCIL—No. 1A]

[*As reported with amendments, recommitted and reported with further amendments, report adopted, Standing Orders suspended and passed remaining stages, 11th October, 1972*]

[Prepared by the Hon. C. M. Hill, M.L.C.]

1972

##

A BILL FOR

An Act to amend the Criminal Law Consolidation Act, 1935-1971, and for other purposes.

[   ]

BE IT ENACTED by the Governor of the State of South Australia, with the advice and consent of the Parliament thereof, as follows:

1. (1) This Act may be cited as the "Criminal Law Consolidation Act Amendment Act, 1972". *Short titles.*

(2) The Criminal Law Consolidation Act, 1935-1971, as amended by this Act, may be cited as the "Criminal Law Consolidation Act, 1935-1972".

(3) The Criminal Law Consolidation Act, 1935-1971, is hereinafter referred to as "the principal Act".

2. Section 3 of the principal Act is amended by striking out from the heading commencing "*Unnatural Offences*" the passage "(Sections 69-72)" and inserting in lieu thereof the passage "(Sections 68a-72)". *Arrangement of Act.*

3. The following section is enacted and inserted in the part of the principal Act headed "*Unnatural Offences*" immediately before section 69 thereof:— *Enactment of s. 68a of principal Act—*

The Death of Dr Duncan

It was potent stuff and helpful, especially for CAMP whose members were committed to advancing law reform. The Duncan case was dropping the issue straight into their laps.

Yet the editorial was topped five days later by an unexpected announcement from a member of the Upper House, Murray Hill. Hill was from the Liberal and Country League Party, the conservative side of politics, then in opposition against the Labor Party headed by Don Dunstan. Hill revealed that he would prepare a private member's bill (that is, without the formal backing of his party) to enact decriminalisation – something that not even the Labor Party had been able to achieve. It would eventually be introduced within 11 weeks of Duncan's death.

Hill said that his legislation would 'seek to protect the privacy only of those people who lived together', and 'certainly would not seek to put the seal of moral approval on homosexuality as such, nor would it condone this sort of behaviour'. It seemed that two homosexual men might finally be able to have sex without intrusion into the privacy of their own homes, but they should not forget they were social outcasts. This is not to criticise Hill, who very likely was trying to make the Bill palatable to members of his own side of politics, and from whom he probably was coming under intense scrutiny. Hill was interviewed by an ABC journalist who asked the astounding question: 'You're not a homosexual yourself?' Hill didn't flinch before answering in the negative. He was married with a family, one child of whom was Robert, a junior solicitor who would help draft the Bill. Murray Hill demonstrated courage and leadership, and is the hero of the piece in relation to the law reform events of 1972.

Hill's Bill for 'An Act to amend the Criminal Law Consolidation Act 1935–1971, and for other purposes' was introduced into the Legislative Council on 26 July. The Council was dominated by Liberal and Country League members who were mostly rural and heavily conservative. The Council operated under an outdated gerrymander such that in 1972 the Labor Party held only four of 20 seats. Four days earlier the *Sunday Mail*'s political correspondent, 'Onlooker', had predicted the Bill would never pass, citing a voting pattern of 11 firmly against, six for and three undecided. Parliamentarians in both houses did not have to vote along party lines but would be allowed a free vote according to their conscience. This was agreed upon by the leader of the Liberal and Country League Party, Dr Bruce Eastick, and Don Dunstan for the Labor Party. Even so, CAMP was advised the Bill would have an easy run in the House of Assembly, which Labor controlled.

CAMP decided to lobby hard for the Bill, but it was seen only as an interim measure. The group hoped that the Mitchell Committee would recommend wider reform. On the morning of 2 August, the group joined the deputations of supporters and

The Death of Dr Duncan

CAMP newsletter calling for gay law reform

opponents who swamped Hill, just before the Bill was to receive its second reading. CAMP was led by Keith Seaman (a future South Australian Governor) and Bill Bennetts – Methodist and Anglican clergymen respectively, which lent its submission a religious air. Clearly this was meant to counterbalance the delegations from religious groups like the Community Standards Organisation and Moral Re-Armament, who were strongly opposed.

Hill was one of the most progressive members of the Liberal and Country League Party. But the Bill was not a charter for gay liberation and very unlike the 1975 Bill which created full legal parity for all regardless of sexuality. Hill distanced himself as a spokesman for any homosexual rights group and CAMP was mentioned only once in his introductory speech. Indeed, he quoted the Moral Freedom Committee in his first parliamentary sentence, and he later described the group as 'not homosexuals; they are young, educated and intelligent South Australians who are taking a great interest in an extremely important social issue. They are thinkers; they are our leaders of the future'.

The Bill was based on that introduced into the British Parliament in 1967. It would allow consensual sexual acts in private between two men over the age of 21, even though females could consent to sexual activity in South Australia at the age of 17 and the legal age of adulthood in the state was 18. The Bill defined 'in private' as involving no more than two people and not 'in a lavatory to which the public have or are permitted to have access', a specific reference to beats. Hill would later admit that the Bill was designed so that homosexuals would be 'less subject to harassment in private, therefore, I believe that there will be less behaviour of this kind in public places such as the Torrens bank'.

CAMP attacked the privacy clause, pointing out: 'It would be quite wrong to suggest that the presence of, say, four guests in the dining room of a private home converted [it] into a public place.' The group also protested at the provisions of the Bill which prescribed a three-year jail term for 'procuring' or 'attempting to procure' a homosexual act. This would condone police crackdowns, not just on beats but anywhere homosexuals congregated publicly: 'The homosexual couple … cannot even get to base since virtually any human act involving two persons must surely be preceded by some invitation, suggestion, or request, whether verbal or otherwise.' But at this early stage Hill was not prepared to make any alterations.

In his speech introducing the Bill into the Legislative Council, Hill said he had acted 'as a result of deep concern regarding the recent death of Dr Duncan'. He concluded:

> In this state, a challenge has come to our often expressed claims, that we, within the nation as a whole, are a tolerant

1972 Decriminalisation Bill

and socially understanding people; that challenge came as a result of the Duncan inquiry and the public discussion that followed.

Other parliamentarians joined to confirm what a powerful catalyst Duncan's killing had been for law reform. For example, David Tonkin, the Liberal and Country League member who introduced the Bill into the House of Assembly, declared that 'the whole subject of homosexual behaviour was brought to the fore again in this state with the tragic death of Dr Duncan'. But others argued that this was not a compelling reason to proceed. The Shadow Attorney-General, Robin Millhouse, claimed that the 'heightened emotion' of the issue was 'not the atmosphere in which we should hastily change the law'.

Duncan's death and the resultant Bill had indeed happened so quickly that CAMP had limited time not just to lobby but to educate members of parliament about this bold piece of social legislation. This became apparent as parliamentary debate commenced, with even those in support delivering speeches which only served to stigmatise further an already marginalised group. Murray Hill resorted to clunky metaphor when he referred to: 'These odd men out, these men with a limp, [who] wait for help on the roadside of life.' He admitted that he hoped the Bill might 'encourage some people to come into the open and seek treatment'. Another parliamentarian declared that 'like alcoholism, mental derangement and adultery, this is not a palatable subject to discuss', adding: 'I have much sympathy for these people, whatever their frailty might be.' The (Catholic) Attorney-General, Len King, said male homosexual acts were a 'perverted activity' and 'intrinsically evil', even though he supported the Bill.

Parliamentarians who spoke against took a harder line, believing that it could be seen as making homosexuality socially acceptable. One commented that he was concerned 'about the many people who could be influenced into this sort of practice'. Another confirmed: 'I believe that anything we do to relax the laws on homosexuality will tend to increase its incidence.' He further inflamed the debate by stating: 'I was recently told that male teachers in certain schools were soliciting the agreement of senior, even junior, male students to commit homosexual acts.' Adelaide's populace would make the connection between homosexuality and paedophilia in the *Advertiser* the following morning. There were even fears expressed – presciently, as it transpired – that homosexual marriage would follow, though that parliamentarian gave it only 10 years.

Members of parliament were inundated with letters from the public, as were the media. Of many letters to the editor published by the *Advertiser* on the subject, those in favour were overwhelmed by those against who mainly justified their position using religious arguments. Anne E. Joyce said: 'God, in his Holy Word, has set down moral rules for mankind, and if man deliberately and defiantly disobeys, then he will destroy himself.' Mary Jonats read the story at breakfast and declared: 'I could not swallow my food nor the Bill.' But Margaret Ferrie called the scriptures 'an historical account of bygone centuries' and asked: 'Surely there is such a thing as progress and reform.' She was backed up by CAMP's Roger Knight who argued that the views of Old Testament fundamentalists should not be 'the basis for law-making in a secular society'.

CAMP was busy working behind the scenes to get the Bill passed, but not all homophile groups supported it. Gay Liberation, for example, operating more from a revolutionary than reformist position, argued that only full legal equality for homosexuals was acceptable. It condemned the Bill as 'totally inadequate and probably even dangerous'.

On 11 October the Legislative Council voted 9-6 in support of the second reading of the Bill. The only Labor member against was Tom Casey, Minister of Agriculture and Forests. One Liberal and Country League member tried a delaying tactic by pushing for the establishment of a Select Committee, but this was defeated. The Bill now entered into the Committee stage where Ren DeGaris – the leader of the Conservatives in the Legislative Council – introduced a devastating amendment. DeGaris had earlier written to CAMP warning of the 'social evils stemming from homosexuality'. He moved that a private, consensual act, committed between two men over 21, would exist only as a defence in court. He stated: 'I am persuaded that if we are to make legislative progress we should not legalise the act in certain circumstances, but should provide a defence if certain conditions exist.' It was a brilliant but cruel political tactic. It allowed for a measure of reform, inevitable and perhaps even necessary after the death of Dr Duncan, but meant that homosexual men would still be dragged before the courts with the attendant publicity. A Labor member of the Upper House complained that the amendment 'would run right across the spirit of the Bill'. The *Advertiser* editorialised against the move, arguing that it would require homosexuals 'to reveal details of their sexual behaviour in court'. The amendment, however, was carried on a voice vote.

The Chief Secretary now moved to reduce the age of consent to 18 but was defeated 12-3. Hill then introduced further amendments 'because people have queried the Bill and sought further clarification'. CAMP's lobbying on the procurement provisions had been successful. The final amended Bill just passed its third reading in the Legislative Council on an 8-6 vote.

The Bill then moved to the House of Assembly where debate occurred in one sitting on the night of 18 October. Labor under Dunstan's leadership stuck to its promise as the Bill was debated in under four hours and opposed only by Liberal

1972 Decriminalisation Bill

and Country League members. David Tonkin enthusiastically supported its passage in a long speech, even arguing for an age of consent of 18, while still describing homosexuality as 'an abnormal emotional attachment'. Nevertheless, on the whole, Lower House parliamentarians indulged in less emotive and ill-informed rhetoric than their Upper House colleagues. Dunstan made clear for the first time that South Australian police engaged in entrapment to snare homosexuals, a point supported by a colleague who accused Vice Squad officers of persecuting homosexuals 'with the aim of getting money from them to hush them up'. Even Attorney-General King described police methods as 'repulsive, intolerable, and indeed counter-productive'.

In Committee stage Labor moved successfully to restore the Bill to its original charter, but also reduced the age of consent to 18. This move was doubly provocative to its opponents in the Legislative Council. CAMP had to work hard before the return of the Bill to the Upper House the following Wednesday. A letter was sent to all Councillors imploring them to accept the amendments, including the reduced age of consent. A circular was also issued to all members urging them to barrage parliamentarians with letters of support.

But there was little joy for CAMP. On 25 October Hill raised the age of consent back to 21 before the Council voted 8-6 to reject the House of Assembly's amendments. It was clear that the Legislative Council would never pass the Bill in its original form and CAMP realised that the DeGaris amendment – while highly unsatisfactory – would be an improvement on the previous draconian legislation. The Bill with the amendment was passed that night and assented to by the governor on 9 November. A CAMP spokesman was quoted describing developments as 'unsatisfactory, but part way to our objective'. With seven of the 10 Legislative Councillors who voted against the Bill up for re-election in March 1973, plans would soon be underway for another attempt at decriminalisation.

This would be another private member's bill but of a fundamentally different nature, introduced by a Labor member into the House of Assembly. It would also be doomed to fail.

CHAPTER 9

1973 and 1975 Decriminalisation Bills

CAMP maintained its reformist political agenda in the shadow of the debilitating amendment to Murray Hill's 1972 Bill. It took advantage of the launch of its book, *Homosexuality in South Australia*, to reiterate its concern that the new law was 'highly unsatisfactory' and 'a thoroughly illusory measure of reform'. Further motivation came with the announcement of a state election for 10 March 1973, and the possibility of a reduction in the Liberal and Country League's majority in the Legislative Council. Letters were dispatched to Anglican clergy in Adelaide, claiming 'the case for a thorough reform of the law is as strong now as it was six months ago'. A press statement denounced the two major parties for their failure to include law reform in their policy platforms. It called not only for decriminalisation but also the outlawing of discrimination against homosexuals in the State Public Service and the areas of employment and housing, and the official recognition of same-sex couples. This was a surprisingly wide-ranging, even radical, set of demands by the organisation. It had been produced by CAMP's public relations officer, Jon Ruwolt.

CAMP was not the only group challenging society's thinking on homosexuality. A South Australian branch of Gay Liberation, inaugurated on 23 August 1972, was now meeting weekly and publishing a fortnightly newsletter. Focusing on consciousness-raising, Gay Liberation stressed 'individual discovery of total personality by discussion and involvement with others'; homosexuals could either be 'victims' or 'rebels', and only a radical transformation of society would eliminate its heterosexist basis. This appealed to women members of CAMP who believed Gay Liberation was more prepared to challenge both sexism and heterosexism. Tensions began to arise between an organisation that operated within the system and one that wanted to smash the system. An editorial in CAMP's magazine *Canary* called for 'greater understanding, tolerance and cooperation between the homosexual movements around Australia'.

Matters came to a head when Ruwolt suddenly declared he was leaving CAMP, followed by the announcement of the formation of the Gay Activists Alliance (GAA), with him as spokesman. What followed was an attack on a 'vague and formless' movement, with Gay Liberation criticised for its failure 'to put ideology into action', and CAMP for its alienation of women and a disposition merely for 'discussion or socialising'. GAA's program for 'Gay Consciousness' would

1973 and 1975 Decriminalisation Bills

emphasise activity in the community based on a more defiantly radical program:

> Without attempting to be reformist, that is, apologetic to the society we inhabit, our aim is to tackle and confront that society with gays as a united force working within it rather than hiding from it. Militant and proud rather than humble and accepting!

GAA quickly became the new public face of an expanded 'gay rights' movement in South Australia, pressing for societal change with a mixture of the broadly liberal, reformist mandate of CAMP, and the more radical, counter-culture focus of Gay Liberation. The organisation met weekly, ran regular consciousness-raising sessions and engaged in public 'zapping' (confronting on their ignorance of homosexuality the entertainer Ernie Sigley, parliamentarian Steele Hall, and Dr John Court from the newly formed South Australian branch of the Festival of Light). GAA also began a program of correspondence with state politicians, the media and clergy, calling for law reform and an end to discrimination. It gained pictorial coverage in the *Advertiser* after demonstrating on the steps of Parliament House during rush hour with members handing out sweets (*Boiled Sweets* was the title of its newsletter) and leaflets which declared: 'Homosexuals are coming out, proud of our sexuality and identity!' GAA activists also addressed medical students and members of Rotoract and were interviewed on radio and television. The name of Gay Activists Alliance said it all, with the movement infused with a new energy and direction.

In November 1972 Murray Hill had written to CAMP advising that 'it would be easier to amend [the] existing Bill rather than to start the process all over again of introducing a new Act'. Asked to comment following the launch of GAA, however, he stated that he would make no such attempt as he did not think 'it would be possible to succeed with a further measure at this stage'. It is likely he was simply being pragmatic. The March election, which had seen half the Legislative Council up for re-election, had reduced the Liberal and Country League majority by only two. It still left the Labor Party with an eight-seat deficit and several implacable opponents. Then, in July 1973, came the sudden announcement that two Labor members of the House of Assembly had 'decided to brave the possible wrath of their constituents, and do something concrete about changes to legislation':

> A Bill to remove the anti-homosexual clauses from the *Criminal Law Consolidation Act* will probably be introduced in the House of Assembly on the twenty-fifth of this month, with the added condition that homosexuality be no longer considered a crime (a safeguard clause, to make sure

1973 and 1975 Decriminalisation Bills

successive Government's [sic] don't revive the Common Law Crime of Buggery).

The proposed legislative changes were even broader, however; a push for the prohibition of discrimination against homosexuals would follow soon after.

While these unexpected developments initially prompted much lobbying of parliamentarians by GAA members, the organisation suddenly withdrew, claiming such activity was not within its ideological purview. Radical lesbians had argued that larger issues were at stake than those addressed in a Bill that favoured only men. In addition, Ruwolt had been advised by Don Dunstan's press secretary, Peter Ward, that the government supported the legislation and GAA should tread carefully to ensure its safe passage. Responsibility for activity transferred to the Committee for Homosexual Law Reform in South Australia, or 'CHARLES', and in a strange irony both poles of the gay rights movement seemed to be voluntarily relinquishing their public roles to achieve reform. CHARLES met twice with the 'heterosexually inclined' and newly elected Labor member for Elizabeth, Peter Duncan, who acted because 'I didn't believe in ... "victimless crimes"'. A 'victimless crime' is one which, 'although an offence, under a statute or at common law, is committed between willing partners or in a situation where there is no person against whom the crime is committed'.

The concept for the new law very likely was based on a proposal put forward by the South Australian Council for Civil Liberties. Peter Duncan introduced his Bill for 'An Act to amend the Criminal Law Consolidation Act, 1935–1972, and the Police Offences Act, 1953–1972' into the House of Assembly on 19 September 1973, appropriately following Adelaide's first Gay Pride Week. In what has been described as a 'trail-blazing' law for Australia, the Bill provided for 'a code of sexual behaviour' applicable to all persons regardless of sex or sexual orientation. In creating statutory equality between homosexuals and heterosexuals, it established a common age of consent of 17 (compared with 21 for homosexual activity resulting from the 1972 Bill), the same penalties for non-consenting acts and the same restrictions on public acts and penalties. It abolished the offences of buggery, gross indecency and soliciting for homosexual purposes, but now recognised male prostitution and homosexual rape. Harsh penalties were prescribed for sexual offences against children, with special reference to those committed by teachers, guardians or others in a duty of care. This indeed was far-sighted legislation, and not only in the gains it made for homosexuals:

> Its wider significance ... lies in the example it set to other Australian states of a more rational approach to regulating

1973 and 1975 Decriminalisation Bills

sexual behaviour, removing unnecessary distinctions in the way the law treated homosexual and heterosexual behaviour, and limiting the scope for double-standards in the way that men's and women's sexual conduct is viewed by the law.

In the second reading of the Bill, Peter Duncan argued precisely that 'the law in this area is entirely inconsistent and not based on sound legal principles'. While he stressed that the proposed decriminalisation of homosexual acts should not 'be highlighted and given great prominence, at the expense of other provisions' of the legislation, his wide-ranging and cogent speech concentrated almost entirely on the subject, as did the *Advertiser*'s reporting. He confirmed, however, that the Bill was in no way to be seen as condoning homosexual practices or behaviours in public, and made no mention of any homosexual reform groups. Nevertheless, CAMP was coordinating its own campaign, on the basis the Bill would probably pass the Assembly but was two votes short of a majority in the Legislative Council. The plan was to target Tom Casey and Ross Story, whose voting intentions at this stage were uncertain.

As CAMP had predicted the Bill was passed in the lower chamber and quickly; involving only five speakers in two weeks a division was not even called for the vote. But on 1 November the *Advertiser* reported that GAA proposed 'to give talks on homosexuality to SA secondary school students from next year', with Jon Ruwolt confirming that they would address only Leaving and Matriculation students. The Minister of Education, Hugh Hudson, stated that in line with the government's policy of autonomy for individual schools, 'I have every confidence in their ability to ensure that on controversial questions the students are able to consider all points of view'. The issue erupted in both Houses of Parliament that afternoon, with one member of the House of Assembly quoting an editorial in the *News* that the 'proper place for children to learn about homosexuality is in carefully researched sex education classes which present a balanced view by people trained in the profession of teaching'. An exasperated Hudson accused the press of being obsessed with sex and advised that he would not issue a directive to schools, no matter what the outcome of Duncan's Bill. GAA was unrepentant, attending at the *Advertiser* offices that evening to argue its case.

However, debate on the Bill in the Legislative Council, which had commenced on 10 October, now soured. Councillors were convinced that gay activists were enjoining more people to their cause. Gordon Gilfillan claimed that GAA planned to 'promote' its activities in schools. Richard Geddes stated that while initially he was in favour, 'thanks to the Gay Activist[s] Alliance, I [will] oppose the Bill'. Tom Casey, whose vote CAMP had determined as being crucial, said:

1973 and 1975 Decriminalisation Bills

> I emphasize very strongly indeed that homosexuality is not, as certain Gay Activist groups would have it, the life style of the future ... I believe that under existing legislation homosexuals have a freedom which has been denied to them for many years ... To go further (as is attempted in this Bill) will put our youth and moral decency that we respect in our community at a distinct disadvantage. It is for those reasons that I cannot support the Bill.

On 21 November the Bill was put to the vote on the second reading and defeated on the casting vote of the President, Sir Lyell McEwin. In an astonishing lapse a Labor member, Cec Creedon, who supported the Bill (together with three Liberal and Country League members and one Liberal Movement member), failed to vote. He claimed he had not heard the bells ringing for the division. But Brian Chatterton, who had introduced the Bill into the Council, had a fallback position. He called up a curious and rarely used Standing Order (supposedly last employed in 1884) which allowed a Bill defeated at the second reading to be restored to the notice paper. Exactly one week before, however, a new law had been proclaimed which provided the Council's President not only with a casting vote, but also a deliberative vote. McEwin's opposition to the Bill was well known and Labor 'unknowingly ... handed [him] an obstructionist weapon'. The Bill lapsed on a tied vote, defeated for the second time. The *Advertiser* editorialised:

There are two unfortunate consequences of Sir Lyell's action. One is that a desirable, and inevitable, legal reform has been delayed. The other is that attention may once more be focused on the Council as a reactionary body. Even Labor propaganda could not be as damaging in this respect as last week's episode.

It seemed clear that a further attempt at law reform would meet solid opposition from Liberal and Country League members in the Legislative Council. Any changes to the voting pattern of the chamber were not likely to occur until the next election, due to be held in 1976. Peter Duncan had stated that he intended to reintroduce the Bill in the next session of parliament in mid-1974, prompting the Festival of Light to circularise its members with a petition for both Houses of Parliament calling for a referendum on the issue. CAMP member Roger Knight proposed yet another committee to argue for law reform and involving representatives from 'the professions and churches'. He claimed that 'no useful purpose would be served by connecting such a projected committee with either CAMP or any other of the specifically homosexual pressure groups in Adelaide'. In March, GAA confirmed the Bill's forthcoming submission, and in a furious denunciation of Dr Court and state politicians declared: 'If Parliamentarians will not support homosexual people, Parliament deserves to be overthrown and replaced by some system of government that will.'

1973 and 1975 Decriminalisation Bills

But nothing came of these developments, and advocacy for gay rights in South Australia now started to flounder. At a 'poorly attended' meeting of CAMP in March 1974, it was decided to continue as an organisation, but by mid-year it essentially was moribund. GAA strove to deliver a more revolutionary message. There were weekly gatherings of 'Radicalesbians' and Gay Liberation; an 'effeminist manifesto' was released together with a weighty submission on health education in schools; and Jon Ruwolt established the first gay and lesbian bookshop – the Dr Duncan Revolution Bookshop – in the front room of his North Adelaide home. But the organisation faded away, as with similar groups in Melbourne and Sydney. Yet much was suddenly happening to engage the movement. The American Psychiatric Association announced that it had removed homosexuality from its list of mental disorders, the Australian Psychological Society publicly condemned discrimination against homosexuals, and a poll in the *Bulletin* declared 'the public is 2-to-1 for legalising homosexual acts'. In South Australia the Labor Party formally declared its support for law reform at a meeting of its State Council in June 1974. But it would be another year before a further attempt at decriminalisation would be made.

An election was suddenly called and held on 12 July 1975. The Dunstan Government was returned to power and, while commanding only a one-seat majority in the House of

Assembly, its representation in the Legislative Council changed dramatically. Under a more democratic electoral system half the Council had faced the polls and there were eight new members, six of them with the Labor Party. The state of the parties was now: Labor – 10; Liberal – nine (the Liberal and Country League Party had renamed itself the Liberal Party of Australia (SA Division)); and Liberal Movement – two. This was described as 'not a government majority but a majority for electoral reform'. In addition, three opponents of gay law reform, including Sir Lyell McEwin, were no longer in the chamber.

This was enough for Peter Duncan to declare on 7 August that he would reintroduce his Bill to enact decriminalisation, an announcement welcomed by the *Advertiser*: 'In the light of modern community attitudes it would be deplorable if the State Parliament again failed to give effect to what is now clearly desired by general public opinion.' Some of its readers did not agree, however, warning that the state would 'sink further into the quicksand of Sodom-like depravity' and claiming that homosexuals were 'a proselytizing sect of anti-social sexual deviants'. The Festival of Light joined the offensive, urging its members to oppose the Bill with a letter-writing campaign and repeating its 1973 call for a referendum in a nine-page submission to state parliament.

1973 and 1975 Decriminalisation Bills

HOUSE OF ASSEMBLY

[*As laid on the table and read a first time, 27th August, 1975*]

[Prepared by Mr. P. Duncan, M.P.]

1975

****

A BILL FOR **No. 14**

An Act to amend the Criminal Law Consolidation Act, 1935-1974, and the Police Offences Act, 1953-1974.

[   ]

BE IT ENACTED by the Governor of the State of South Australia, with the advice and consent of the Parliament thereof, as follows:

1. This Act may be cited as the "Criminal Law (Sexual Offences) Amendment Act, 1975". *Short title.*

PART I

AMENDMENT OF THE CRIMINAL LAW CONSOLIDATION ACT, 1935-1974

2. (1) The Criminal Law Consolidation Act, 1935-1974, as amended by this Act, may be cited as the "Criminal Law Consolidation Act, 1935-1975". *Short titles.*

(2) The Criminal Law Consolidation Act, 1935-1974, is in this Part referred to as "the principal Act".

3. Section 3 of the principal Act is amended by striking out from the heading "*Rape, Defilement and Abduction of Women and Girls* (Sections 48-68)" the passage "*of Women and Girls*". *Amendment of principal Act, s. 3— Arrangement of Act.*

4. Section 5 of the principal Act is amended by inserting in subsection (1) after the last definition contained therein the following definitions:— *Amendment of principal Act, s. 5— Interpretation.*

"common prostitute" includes any male person who prostitutes his body for fee or reward:

"rape" includes *penetratio per anum* of a male person without his consent.

5. The heading "*Rape, Defilement and Abduction of Women and Girls*" immediately preceding section 48 of the principal Act is amended by striking out the passage "*of Women and Girls*". *Amendment of heading preceding s. 48 of principal Act.*

H.A.—21

1975 Bill

The Death of Dr Duncan

The Bill, almost identical in legal intent to that of 1973, was debated in the House of Assembly on 27 August 1975. The new Opposition Leader, Dr David Tonkin, who had introduced the 1972 Hill Bill into the Lower House, was in support; seven political allies from rural electorates were not, with one attempting to adjourn proceedings, which would likely have seen the Bill lapse. But debate was brisk and in the same sitting the Bill passed the second reading by a majority of 23, supported by every Labor member and nine members of the Liberal Party – including both its present and former leaders, and the leader of the Liberal Movement, Robin Millhouse. It was eventually carried on a voice vote.

Millhouse was forced publicly to defend his stance but was able to rely on an unexpected player who had entered the arena, and who now gave the Bill impetus as it was sent to the Legislative Council. On 1 September the newly appointed Anglican Archbishop of Adelaide, the Most Reverend Dr Keith Rayner, touched on gay law reform in a wide-ranging pastoral address to his first diocesan synod:

> Personally I favour it, not because I condone homosexual acts, but because I believe that the sanctions of criminal law are not the best way of dealing with the deep and complex problems associated with homosexuality.

1973 and 1975 Decriminalisation Bills

Rayner's support was qualified, for he was critical of what he perceived as the 'glorification' of homosexual life and stressed that homosexual partnerships were not analogous to heterosexual marriage. But the *Advertiser* was quick to seize on the statement, giving it prominence in a page-one article headed 'Archbishop favors move'.

This development coincided propitiously with the release to Legislative Councillors of a document, 'A Matter of Social Concern', by a group styling itself the 'Social Concern Committee'. The document, which included 13 pages of appendices, was divided into seven sections: An Important Social Reform; The Present Law and Psychiatric Assistance; The Present Law and Violence; The Present Law in Disrepute; Wide-spread Community Support for Reform; A Safe Reform; and A Moderate, Cautious Reform. It argued that the proposed reforms:

> simply decriminalise homosexual behaviour and do not imply that such behaviour is either 'normal' or 'natural'. The acceptability of homosexual behaviour is something for modern society to decide upon, not the function of the criminal law.

One of its authors later admitted that what the document 'skirted around really carefully was ... the okayness of gayness ...

Whenever that issue emerged the Social Concern Committee galloped away in the opposite direction.'

'A Matter of Social Concern' was still a convincing rebuttal of the earlier submission to parliament by the religious opposition, the Festival of Light and the Community Standards Organisation. Once again, the involvement of gay lobbyists – reformist or radical – was eschewed in favour of prominent clergy, psychologists, social workers and academics, headed by the redoubtable the Reverend Keith Seaman. With support for law reform now offered by representatives of the Anglican, Catholic, Congregational and Methodist denominations, the Festival of Light was directly challenged in its claim that it represented the unanimous Christian view. On the basis that the full committee had not actually convened (the bulk of its work having been done by small subgroups), Dr Court on radio tried to denounce the committee as a fraud, and in desperation produced a further personal submission to Councillors.

As the Bill entered the Upper House on 9 September, letters calling for reform were also arriving from the South Australian Council for Civil Liberties and a local branch of the Australian Psychological Society. In her introductory speech the recently elected Anne Levy was now able to list in detail the influential churches, community groups, newspapers, political and professional organisations and public polls that supported the legislation. She also worked to dismiss one of the central arguments of the Festival of Light and conservative opponents of the Bill, who had maintained that it would lead to the destruction of the family unit in society:

> If objectors to this Bill were really consistent in their concern for maintaining family life, they should try to have adultery and fornication made crimes ... Adultery will always cause far more marriages to founder than will homosexual practices, as our divorce courts have shown only too well.

Opposing Councillors, now faced with the Archbishop's statement, the Social Concern Committee and the lack of any contentious lobbying by gay organisations, resorted to quoting from their 1973 parliamentary speeches, including raising the spectre of the now defunct Gay Activists Alliance. Also galling for them were the actions of Labor's Norm Foster, who interrupted an impassioned speech to point his finger at the Opposition benches and boom: 'How do I know that honourable members do not indulge, and how do they know that I do not?'

But after the Bill had passed comfortably its second reading by eight votes (with support from five Liberal Party and Liberal Movements members), John Burdett moved for amendments in Committee. These would have made it an offence to advocate or encourage 'any unnatural sexual practice' within the precincts of a school or in advertisements, with a penalty of a fine of up to $1000 or six months' imprisonment. It was a clever ploy as it played upon Councillors' continued unease from the 1973 debate of homosexuals 'proselytising' their views; Labor's Chris Sumner admitted that he had 'a considerable amount of sympathy for the intention of the mover'. The Bill was now in danger of lapsing if the amendments divided its advocates. Two second-reading supporters defected over the amendments, which were defeated by only two votes; the third reading resolved 12 to six in favour, with the only Labor member against being the 'particularly homophobic' Tom Casey.

The Bill formally passed on 17 September 1975 and was assented to the following day; it became law on 25 September. The lack of direct, and contentious, gay lobbying (indeed, virtually the lack of an organised gay rights movement), combined with an astutely formed outside committee and the unexpected pronouncements of a newly appointed Anglican archbishop, overcame major religious opponents finally to achieve reform. This was not only a first for South Australia and Australia. It was also the first legislation in the English-speaking world to eliminate any distinction in the criminal law between heterosexual and homosexual, including an equal age of consent. CAMP declared its delight at the passing of the Bill, saying the organisation hoped 'to educate the public about homosexuality and secure a community acceptance of homosexual people'. Dr Court's response was to proclaim that moves to decriminalise bestiality may be next.

1973 and 1975 Decriminalisation Bills

South Australia's lead was soon followed by the Australian Capital Territory (1976), then Victoria (1980), the Northern Territory (1983), New South Wales (1984), Western Australia (1989), Queensland (1990) and, finally, Tasmania in 1997.

There is a fascinating postscript to South Australia's story. On 9 October 1975, Peter Duncan, who was aged only 30, became South Australia's 42nd Attorney-General. But within three weeks he found himself confronting calls for his resignation in the House of Assembly. It was claimed he had told a meeting of the New South Wales Council for Civil Liberties that he supported homosexuals being allowed to address children in classrooms. This directly contradicted a statement he made when introducing the Bill. Duncan was forced to deny that he had deliberately misled parliament when the ABC reported that he had admitted this statement would ensure the Bill's passage.

The Minister of Education, Don Hopgood, issued a press release asserting that he was opposed to any such move, and Duncan was summoned by Premier Dunstan for an explanation. An *Advertiser* editorial described Duncan's behaviour as 'irresponsible', and even the usually on-side *Nation Review* argued that a *prima facie* case seemed to exist against him. When the Opposition threatened to call people before the Bar of Parliament in an attempt to have the transcript of the interview made public, the ABC responded that – in line with

The Death of Dr Duncan

policy – it would not release the notes. Duncan tried valiantly to defend his position, declaring he was originally referring specifically to homosexuals preaching their views. In the end he survived the motion calling for his resignation, but only on the casting vote of the Speaker.

Conclusion

On 10 May 2022 it will be 50 years since Dr Duncan's drowning. It is an anniversary that South Australia justly will commemorate. But there is an intense poignancy – for some a deep sadness, even anger – knowing that the people who threw him to his death remain unconvicted. It is more than a matter of profound regret that suspicions of police involvement have not been dulled by time.

The Duncan case is a reminder of the social opprobrium that attached (and, regrettably, still does for some people) to male homosexuality. That a state-funded apparatus operated – with the potential for imprisonment – to entrap and brutalise homosexuals is a powerful commentary on the irrational fear that then existed around a sexual minority. Also, of the appalling situation that allowed such conduct to permeate an agency whose primary role should have been to protect its citizens, not attack them. And, if Mick O'Shea is to be believed, that permitted those attackers to brag about their activities in their workplace.

The Death of Dr Duncan

In engaging in their corrupt and morally bankrupt behaviour, those members of South Australia's Vice Squad who terrorised homosexuals on the Torrens riverbank were themselves criminals. They and any of their superiors who either encouraged it or turned a blind eye should have been the ones jailed, not the men whose sexual orientation marked them as social pariahs or, worse, perverts. Not the 'poofters', 'fags' or 'fairies' – and these are the polite terms – who were labelled and condemned by society's intolerance and hostility, which could border on hatred.

The Duncan case garnered publicity mainly because he was a member of a respected profession, and one related to the law. He may have had no family or few friends – no one reported him missing after all – but he was defended by his colleagues while a horrified community demanded answers. What would have happened had he been a working-class man, with no one around possessing the media nous and legal savvy to defend him? The case may never have gained the traction it did.

The exceptionally quick parliamentary response to Duncan's drowning, led by Murray Hill from the conservative side of politics, was laudable. Still, I have argued that the 1972 decriminalisation Bill:

> was not meant to bring homosexuals into parity with heterosexuals within the wider community. It was aimed

Conclusion

at reducing blackmail, keeping the police force out of decoy activities and allowing homosexuals to seek 'treatment'. Most importantly, it ensured that homosexuality was removed to the private sphere and out of the public eye ...

It was, however, an important and brave beginning. Three years later South Australia would embrace pioneering legislation that delivered equality in the criminal law regardless of gender or sexuality. For this we have to thank Peter Duncan and Anne Levy, the Labor Party led by Don Dunstan, and some courageous members from the Opposition benches. It is extraordinary to consider that the last Australian jurisdiction to enact gay law reform – Tasmania – would take another 22 years.

Dr Duncan has not been forgotten. In March 2002 a committee from the local rainbow community led by the Australian Democrats parliamentarian Sandra Kanck unveiled a memorial plaque to Duncan at the southern entrance to the University of Adelaide footbridge. In 2015 Duncan's original employer, what is now the Adelaide Law School at the University of Adelaide, established the Dr Duncan Memorial Scholarship. On 20 July 2020 – the 90th anniversary of Duncan's birth – the Adelaide City Council, again adjacent to the footbridge, unveiled an interpretive sign. Duncan also features as part of the Council's Pride Walk in Light Square in the city.

The Death of Dr Duncan

In March 2022 the Adelaide Festival mounted a specially commissioned oratorio, *Watershed: The Death of Dr Duncan*. This book has been published to coincide with the new work, as well as a range of commemorative events which will be held in the lead-up to and around the May anniversary date.

It is one of the many ironies of the Duncan case that this public recognition is something he would have abhorred. He was an extremely shy, intensely private and taciturn man who may never have identified publicly as homosexual. And yet he has become a gay martyr, a 'queer icon' in modern-day parlance. I can hear him muttering darkly from the grave at the use of such labels.

If he is an icon it is not because of his own actions but of the people – his cowardly killers – who thought it was sport to throw poofters into the Torrens and then flee as they sank to the riverbed. I am the person most responsible for placing Dr Duncan on a pedestal that would not have been of his choosing. I ask now that he be remembered as more than just an epithet.

A Pictorial Record of the Duncan Case 1972–2022

1972 Inquest

THE LAWYERS

Counsel assisting the Coroner,
Rod Matheson

Counsel representing the
University of Adelaide,
Bruce Debelle

1972 Inquest

Counsel representing Mr X,
Derrance Stevenson

Counsel representing
Cawley, Clayton and Hudson,
Bob McRae

1972 Inquest

THE
KEY
WITNESS

Roger James

1972 Inquest

THE
GOOD
SAMARITAN

Bevan Spencer von Einem

1972 Inquest

OTHER WITNESSES

Kevin Williamson

Constable Ronald Harris

1972 Inquest

Constables Martin Maynard and Darryl Smedley

THE EVENTUAL WHISTLEBLOWER

Constable Michael O'Shea

1972 Inquest

SENIOR POLICE

Inspector Colin Lehmann

Police Commissioner Harold Salisbury and
Deputy Commissioner Laurence Draper

1972 Inquest

THE THREE VICE SQUAD OFFICERS

Senior Constable
Brian Hudson

Constable Michael Clayton

Constable Francis Cawley

1972 Inquest

THE NEWS

Adelaide: Wednesday, July 5, 1972   7c*

Dr. Duncan

TODAY'S picture of the Coroner, Mr. Cleland.

VIOLENCE IN DUNCAN DEATH

But finding open

Dr. George Ian Ogilvie Duncan drowned in the River Torrens on May 10 "due to violence on the part of persons of whose identity there is no evidence."

This was the open finding of the Coroner, Mr. T. E. Cleland, today at the conclusion of the inquest into the death of the 42-year-old Adelaide University law lecturer.

Mr. Cleland said, however, that the inquest could be reopened.

He said anybody who had relevant information to communicate in the case should advise Coroner's Court officers or the police, and it would then be considered whether the inquest should be reopened.

Costly

The new Police Commissioner, Mr. R. Salisbury, and the new Deputy Commissioner, Mr. L. D. Draper, were at the court today for the finding.

Mr. Cleland gave his finding after a two-page summary of the facts included in 255 pages of evidence taken at one of South Australia's longest and most costly inquests.

He introduced his finding with the following comment, which referred to three Vice Squad men:

"At this inquest there was no evidence that during the evening of May 10 any of the three officers was nearer than about 100 yards from the place where Dr. Duncan was thrown into the river, and there is no evidence that any person other than Mr. Jacobs and Mr. Williamson was in the vicinity at the relevant times."

● Police accept Vice Squad man's resignation, Page 5;
Inquest continued, Page 5.

● THE Police Commissioner, Mr. Salisbury (left), at the Coroner's Court today with Deputy Commissioner, Mr. Draper (background), and Insp. C. Lehmann.

THEY'RE OFF TO ENGLAND!

Mr. Anthony Weinglass, of Marion, will soon be re-visiting his sister in London, and his wife, Elvira, will have the chance to see her grandparents in Germany, for the first time.

All because of their exciting win in the 1972 Boat Show lottery last night. First prize was a luxury world cruise.

The 1972 Boat Show co-sponsored by The News broke all previous records. 59,739 people attending.

● Pictures P. 31; other details P. 39.

Inquest finding

1972 New Scotland Yard Report

Chief Superintendent Robert McGowan (second from left) and
Sergeant Charles O'Hanlon (second from right)

New Scotland Yard inquiry failure

1985 Reopening of Case

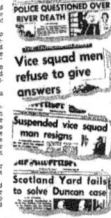

O'Shea speaks out

Cawley, Clayton and Hudson face court

1986 Preliminary Hearing

THE THREE FORMER VICE SQUAD OFFICERS

Cawley

Clayton

Hudson

1986 Preliminary Hearing

Hudson discharged

1988 Trial

Former vice-squad men unlikely to seek Govt compo

By PETER CROOKES

The two former vice-squad detectives found not guilty yesterday of manslaughter over the 1972 drowning of homosexual law lecturer Dr George Duncan are unlikely to seek compensation from the State Government.

Their lawyer said the two men were "just relieved" that the case had ended.

Francis John Cawley, 39, of MacFarlane Street, Glenelg, and Michael Kenneth Clayton, 41, of Mills Street, Clarence Gardens, had pleaded not guilty to having unlawfully killed Dr George Ian Ogilvy Duncan, 42, at the River Torrens on May 10, 1972.

A jury of nine men and three women acquitted the two men after deliberating overnight.

The jury had retired to consider its verdicts at 3.27 p.m. on Thursday and was held in a city hotel overnight before acquitting the two men at 11.05 a.m. yesterday.

It found Clayton not guilty by a unanimous verdict but Cawley was acquitted by a majority verdict of 10 or 11 jurors.

The public gallery of the courtroom was crowded, with about a dozen people standing, when the verdicts ended the 24-day trial.

Mr D. Smith, for Cawley, said outside the court that the verdicts were "justice" ending 16 "very difficult" years for the two former policemen.

"In a way I think they were glad it was all brought to a head," he said.

Mr Smith doubted that either Cawley or Clayton would seek compensation from the State.

As to the Crown charging the men with the manslaughter in February 1986, almost 14 years after the drowning, Mr Smith said the Crown had thought the men had a case to answer.

Both Cawley and Clayton, then constables in the vice-squad, were suspended from the police in 1972 for refusing to answer questions about the drowning.

They also refused to testify at a June 1972 inquest into the drowning, and they resigned from the police shortly after.

Dr Duncan's body was found in the river west of the university footbridge on May 11.

The Crown case was based on allegations that Cawley, Clayton, and two other unidentified men threw Dr Duncan into the River Torrens for amusement as part of "poofter bashing".

But the defence emphasised that no witnesses had testified they saw Cawley and Clayton take part in throwing Dr Duncan into the river.

It argued that the witness descriptions available did not match the two former policemen.

Michael Kenneth Clayton   Francis John Cawley

The defence also attacked the evidence of a key Crown witness, former vice-squad policeman Michael William O'Shea.

O'Shea alleged during the trial that Cawley and Clayton bore an animosity toward homosexuals and bragged about assaulting them, including throwing them in the river.

O'Shea also alleged that senior police covered up the possibility that vice-squad members were involved in the drowning.

Use of illegal search warrants and other allegations of police corruption were also made.

The defence accused O'Shea of lying at the trial as part of his long-standing grudge against the police.

Neither Cawley nor Clayton testified at the trial. They had told police in 1972 that they had briefly been near Jolley's Boathouse on the night of May 10 but knew nothing of Dr Duncan's drowning.

The Crown Prosecutor, Mr P. J. Rice alleged both men lied in the 1972 interviews, the only time they spoke about the drowning.

And he argued that the weight of circumstantial evidence was enough to convict them.

Descriptive evidence from witnesses had not been conclusive but roughly fitted both men.

O'Shea's evidence had shown that Cawley and Clayton had the motive to attack Duncan.

Cawley had cleared the area near Jolley's of uniformed police, asking three police to leave, shortly before the drowning.

He and Clayton had gone to the area with the express purpose of assaulting homosexuals and throwing them into the river, he alleged.

Yesterday's jury decision was greeted with relief by members of the SA Police Force and the acting secretary of the SA Police Association, Mr Peter Parfitt, said the case proved the processes of justice applied to police officers as much as for the public.

"Many members of the force will be pleased with the result which has dispelled any lingering doubt about the veracity of SA police," he said.

"Police do not hold themselves above the law. This will be a boost for us."

Cawley and Clayton acquitted

2002 Release of 1972 New Scotland Yard Report

The Advertiser

Adelaide, Tuesday, July 16, 2002 — Metropolitan Edition — www.theadvertiser.com.au — Phone (08) 8206 2000 — $1.00* including GST

Duncan killing: Scotland Yard report released after 30 years and finds...

VICE POLICE WERE GUILTY

Dr Duncan

Brian Hudson | Michael Clayton | Francis John Cawley

> 124. What really points to their guilt is their actions afterwards. No Police officer would fail to give evidence at an inquest if he had nothing to hide, and we know that they even sacrificed their professional careers in order to maintain their silence.
>
> 129. As I have previously mentioned, there was no real intention of causing anyone's death – this was merely a high-spirited frolic which went wrong, but unless this matter is resolved, justice will not be seen to be done.
>
> – The Scotland Yard Report

DROWNING: Steps lead down to the banks of the River Torrens where Dr George Duncan died, and the three Vice Squad policemen named in the report.

By REX JORY and JEFF TURNER

THREE South Australian policemen caused the death of homosexual academic Dr George Duncan in the River Torrens in 1972, according to a Scotland Yard report.

Prepared by two British detectives in 1972, the report was made public for the first time yesterday in State Parliament by Attorney-General Michael Atkinson.

Dr Duncan had been killed on the night of May 10 that year in a "high-spirited frolic which went wrong", the report says.

The following day, his body was dragged from the River Torrens near a known pick-up area for homosexuals.

The report, prepared by Detective Chief Superintendent Bob McGowan and Detective Sergeant Charles O'Hanlon, examines in detail the events of the night of Dr Duncan's death.

It names three members of the Vice Squad – Constables Francis John Cawley, Michael Kenneth Clayton and Senior Constable Brian Hudson.

In 1988 all three were charged with manslaughter.

Clayton and Cawley were tried and acquitted and Hudson was found to have no case to answer.

In the report, Chief Supt McGowan says, "I (also) believe that the officers mentioned took part, possibly with others, in throwing Duncan, (a witness, Roger Wesley) James and (a third unnamed witness), into the water, but despite intensive inquiries, no further witness has been found who can assist in providing further evidence against them.

"As I have previously mentioned, there was no real intention of causing anyone's death – this was merely a high-spirited frolic which went wrong, but unless this is resolved, justice will not be seen to be done."

Four mystery witnesses, referred to in the report, remain unnamed. Mr Atkinson said they were not public figures.

● Continued Page 4

NEW FALCON – FIRST OFFICIAL PICTURES – PAGE 11

Classifieds Index Page 42 | Call Rhonda on 131 841 | Metro forecast: Early showers, 15° | Index: Page 2

Duncan memorials

Memorial plaque

Pride Walk

Duncan memorials

Interpretive sign

Oratorio

Timeline

1972

10 May	Dr Duncan drowns
20 May	Media revelations that police have been questioned over death
27 May	Place of murder identified as well-known homosexual beat
7 Jun	Inquest commences
21 Jun	Open letter sent to MPs urging decriminalisation of male homosexual acts
29 Jun	Cawley and Clayton refuse to answer questions at inquest
30 Jun	Cawley, Clayton and Hudson suspended from SA Police and later resign
1 Jul	*Advertiser* prints editorial headed 'Legalise Homosexuality'
5 Jul	Coroner finds that Duncan's death was due to violence by persons unknown
6 Jul	Murray Hill announces intention to introduce decriminalisation Bill

26 Jul	Bill introduced into Legislative Council
27 Jul	New Scotland Yard detectives called in to reinvestigate Duncan case
2 Oct	New Scotland Yard report completed; not released publicly until 2002
18 Oct	Significantly weakened Bill introduced into House of Assembly
24 Oct	Announcement that there are inadequate grounds for prosecution from New Scotland Yard report
25 Oct	Amended Bill passes both Houses of Parliament
9 Nov	Bill assented to by Governor

1973

19 Sep	Peter Duncan introduces 1973 Bill into House of Assembly
21 Nov	Bill fails by one vote
28 Nov	Bill reintroduced but defeated again

1975

27 Aug	Peter Duncan introduces 1975 Bill into House of Assembly
17 Sep	Bill passes in state, national and English-speaking world first; assented to following day
25 Sep	Bill becomes law

Timeline

1985

30 Jul   Ex-Vice Squad officer Mick O'Shea claims police cover-up in Duncan case

1 Aug   SA Police reopens Duncan case

1986

5 Feb   Cawley, Clayton and Hudson charged with Duncan's manslaughter

8 Sep   Preliminary hearing commences

29 Oct   Hudson charge dismissed

12 Nov   Cawley and Clayton committed to stand trial

1988

13 Sep   Trial commences

30 Sep   Cawley and Clayton acquitted

1990

3 Apr   'Duncan Task Force Final Report' released

2002

10 May   Memorial plaque unveiled on 30th anniversary of Duncan's death

15 Jul   New Scotland Yard report released publicly

2020

20 Jul   Adelaide City Council interpretive sign unveiled

2021

10 May   Crime Stoppers SA increases reward in Duncan case to $200,000

2022

3 Mar   Adelaide Festival opening night of *Watershed: The Death of Dr Duncan*

2022

10 May   50th anniversary of Duncan's death

Glossary

Abbott QC, Michael
Lawyer who represented **Michael Clayton** at the preliminary hearing

Advertiser
South Australia's morning broadsheet newspaper which covered the Duncan case in-depth; editorialised in support of gay law reform until its success in 1975

Atkinson, Michael
Labor member of the **House of Assembly**; tabled the **New Scotland Yard report** in parliament in 2002

Callaghan, Robert (Bobby)
Claimed to have been with **Dr Duncan** and **Roger James** on the night of the drowning and to have witnessed the attack on them; died before giving evidence at the 1988 trial

Campaign Against Moral Persecution (CAMP)
South Australian branch of national reformist homophile organisation (see **Gay Activists Alliance** and **Gay Liberation**); supported **gay law reform**

Casey, Tom
Member of the **Legislative Council**; the only **Labor** member to vote against the 1972 and 1975 **decriminalisation** Bills

Castles, Professor Alex
Colleague of **Dr Duncan**'s who identified his body

Cawley, Francis
One of three **Vice Squad** officers (see **Clayton, Michael** and **Hudson, Brian**) identified by the **New Scotland Yard report** as being responsible for **Dr Duncan**'s death. Charged with his manslaughter in 1986; acquitted in 1988

City Bridge
The main bridge over the River Torrens; together with the **University of Adelaide footbridge** formed part of the **No. 1 Beat**

Clayton, Michael
One of three **Vice Squad** officers (see **Cawley, Francis** and **Hudson, Brian**) identified by the **New Scotland Yard report** as being responsible for **Dr Duncan**'s death. Charged with his manslaughter in 1986; acquitted in 1988

Cleland, Tom
City Coroner who returned an open finding into **Dr Duncan**'s killing; concluded that Duncan was a homosexual based on **Dr Colin Manock**'s evidence

Committee for Homosexual Law Reform in South Australia (CHARLES)
Independent committee established in 1973; supported **gay law reform**

Community Standards Organisation (CSO)
Conservative Christian lobby group headed by **Dr John Court**; opposed **gay law reform**

Court, Dr John
Senior lecturer in Psychology at Flinders University. Headed the **Community Standards Organisation** and later the **Festival of Light**; opposed **gay law reform**

Glossary

Creedon, Cec
Labor member of the **Legislative Council** whose failure to vote for the 1973 **decriminalisation** Bill led to its ultimate defeat

Debelle, Bruce
Lawyer who represented the **University of Adelaide** (and to protect the reputation of **Dr Duncan**) at the inquest

Decriminalisation
Changing the law so that something is no longer a crime (see **Peter Duncan, Don Dunstan, Murray Hill** and **Anne Levy**)

DeGaris, Ren
Liberal and Country League member and leader of the Conservatives in the **Legislative Council**; introduced the amendment that significantly weakened the 1972 **decriminalisation** Bill

Draper, Laurence
Deputy Police Commissioner

Duncan, Dr George Ian Ogilvie
University of Adelaide law lecturer whose drowning in the River Torrens on 10 May 1972 was the catalyst for **gay law reform** in South Australia

Duncan, Peter
Labor member of the **House of Assembly**, later Attorney-General (not related to Dr Duncan). Introduced **private member's bill**s in 1973 and 1975 – the latter successfully – to enact **gay law reform**

Duncan suitcase
Held **Dr Duncan**'s personal papers (including his correspondence with **Dorothy Glover**) and other material; destroyed by SA Police in 2012

The Death of Dr Duncan

'Duncan Task Force Final Report'
Prepared by SA Police and tabled in the South Australian Parliament in 1990; concluded that there was insufficient evidence to charge any other person with Duncan's death

Dunstan, Don
Labor Premier of South Australia, 1967–68, 1970–79. Unsuccessfully attempted **gay law reform** in 1965; in power when achieved in 1975. Promised anonymity and immunity from prosecution for **Mr X** and **Witnesses B, C and D** in relation to the Duncan case; agreed to the appointment of New Scotland Yard detectives

Eastick, Dr Bruce
Liberal and Country League leader in South Australia; allowed his Party's parliamentarians a conscience vote on the 1972 **decriminalisation** Bill

Festival of Light
Christian lobby group formed out of the **Community Standards Organisation** and headed by **Dr John Court**; opposed **gay law reform**

Foss, Paul
Student newspaper journalist from the Australian National University who covered the Duncan case

Gay Activists Alliance (GAA)
South Australian revolutionary homophile organisation (see **CAMP** and **Gay Liberation**); supported **gay law reform** as part of wider changes to society

Gay law reform
The passing through parliament of legislation involving the **decriminalisation** of male homosexual acts

Glossary

Gay Liberation
South Australian branch of national radical homophile organisation (see **CAMP** and **Gay Activists Alliance**); heavily criticised the 1972 **decriminalisation** Bill

Glover, Dorothy
Piano teacher and organist; fell in love with **Dr Duncan** but was rejected (see **Duncan suitcase**)

Harris, Ronald
Uniformed constable who allegedly was warded off by **Francis Cawley** on the night of **Dr Duncan**'s death

Hill, Murray
Progressive **Liberal and Country League** member of the **Legislative Council**; introduced a **private member's bill** within 11 weeks of Dr Duncan's death to enact **gay law reform**

Hiskey, Garry
Lawyer who represented **Roger James** at the inquest

House of Assembly
The lower (green) chamber in the South Australian Parliament; controlled by the **Labor** Party from 1972 to 1975

Hudson, Brian
One of three **Vice Squad** officers (see **Cawley, Francis** and **Clayton, Michael**) identified by the **New Scotland Yard report** as being responsible for **Dr Duncan**'s death. Charged with his manslaughter in 1986 but not brought to trial

James, Roger
Thrown in with **Dr Duncan** and broke his ankle; said he did not know Duncan and was unable to identify the attackers

King, Len
Labor Attorney-General; supported **gay law reform** in 1972 but described homosexuality as 'intrinsically evil'

Labor
Progressive party of South Australian politics; headed by Premier **Don Dunstan**

Layton, Robyn
Lawyer who represented **Witnesses B, C and D** at the inquest

Legislative Council
The upper (red) chamber in the South Australian Parliament; controlled by the **Liberal and Country League** Party in 1972 and 1973

Lehmann, Inspector Colin
Together with **Inspector Paul Turner** carried out the early police investigation of the Duncan case

Lenton, Superintendent Noel
Head of the Criminal Investigation Bureau to whom **Inspectors Colin Lehmann** and **Paul Turner** reported

Levy, Anne
Labor member who introduced the 1975 **decriminalisation** Bill into the **Legislative Council**

Liberal and Country League (LCL)
Conservative party of South Australian politics that later became the **Liberal Party**; headed in 1972 by **Dr Bruce Eastick** and in 1975 by **Dr David Tonkin**

Liberal Movement (LM)
Progressive political party formed out of the **Liberal and Country League** Party

Liberal Party
Conservative political party formed out of the **Liberal and Country League** Party

Glossary

Lincoln College
Residential college run by the Methodist Church; where **Dr Duncan** lodged in a flat

Lücke, Professor Horst
Law Department head at the **University of Adelaide**; followed the Duncan case closely and acted to protect **Dr Duncan**'s reputation

Manock, Dr Colin
South Australian Director of Forensic Pathology; concluded from his autopsy that **Dr Duncan** was a passive homosexual because of his funnel-shaped anus

Manos, Nick
Magistrate who presided over the 1986 preliminary hearing

Matheson, Rod
Counsel who assisted City Coroner **Tom Cleland** during the inquest; also provided independent opinion on the **New Scotland Yard report**

Maynard, Martin
Uniformed constable who allegedly was warded off by **Francis Cawley** on the night of **Dr Duncan**'s death

McEwin, Sir Lyell
President of the **Legislative Council** whose casting vote led to the defeat of the 1973 **decriminalisation** Bill

McGowan, Chief Superintendent Robert (Bob)
New Scotland Yard detective who with **Charles O'Hanlon** in the **New Scotland Yard report** concluded that **Francis Cawley**, **Michael Clayton** and **Brian Hudson** were guilty of **Dr Duncan**'s killing; later jailed in Britain

McKinna, John
Police Commissioner until replaced by **Harold Salisbury**

McRae, Bob
Lawyer who represented **Francis Cawley**, **Michael Clayton** and **Brian Hudson** at the inquest

Mildenhall, Edwin
Vice Squad officer whose farewell party on the night of **Dr Duncan**'s drowning was attended by **Francis Cawley**, **Michael Clayton** and **Brian Hudson**

Millhouse, Robin
Liberal and Country League member of the **Legislative Council**, later leader of the **Liberal Movement**. Supported the 1975 **decriminalisation** Bill

Mitchell Committee
Established by **Labor** in 1971 to enquire into the state's criminal law, including homosexuality

Moral Action Committee (MAC)
Conservative Christian lobby group; opposed **gay law reform**

Moral Freedom Committee (MFC)
Progressive (and mainly heterosexual) lobby group; supported **gay law reform**

Moral Re-Armament (MRA)
Conservative moral and spiritual lobby group; opposed **gay law reform**

Mr X or Witness A
Unidentified man who was thrown into the **River Torrens** before **Dr Duncan** and **Roger James**; unable to identify his attackers. His name is still protected

New Scotland Yard plaque
Given by SA Police to the New Scotland Yard detectives, **Robert McGowan** and **Charles O'Hanlon**, to record their 'pleasant association' in connection with investigating the Duncan case

Glossary

New Scotland Yard report
Prepared by **Robert McGowan** and **Charles O'Hanlon** of New Scotland Yard after City Coroner **Tom Cleland**'s open finding. Completed in October 1972 but only released publicly on 15 July 2002

No. 1 Beat
A covert meeting place for South Australian homosexual men from before 1910; stretched from **City Bridge** up to and past the **University of Adelaide footbridge**

O'Hanlon, Sergeant Charles
New Scotland Yard detective who with **Robert McGowan** in the **New Scotland Yard report** concluded that **Francis Cawley**, **Michael Clayton** and **Brian Hudson** were guilty of **Dr Duncan**'s killing; later jailed in Britain

O'Loughlin, Justice Maurice
Judge who presided over the 1987 Abuse of Process application and 1988 trial

Osborne, Robert
Was chased from the public toilet on the night of **Dr Duncan**'s drowning

O'Shea, Michael (Mick)
Former **Vice Squad** officer who in 1985 claimed a police cover-up in the Duncan case, leading to its reopening and the eventual charging of **Francis Cawley**, **Michael Clayton** and **Brian Hudson** with **Dr Duncan**'s manslaughter

Preliminary hearing
A hearing to determine whether a *prima facie* case exists to commit a defendant to trial

Private member's bill
A proposed law introduced by a member of parliament without the formal backing of their political party; usually of a socially contentious nature

Rayner, the Most Rev. Dr Keith
Anglican Archbishop of Adelaide; supported the 1975 **decriminalisation** Bill

Review
Left-leaning national newspaper which first revealed the place of murder as a beat and identified **Vice Squad** harassment of homosexuals

Rice, Paul
Crown Prosecutor in the 1986 preliminary hearing and 1988 trial

Ruwolt, Jon
CAMP member; later established **Gay Activists Alliance**

Salisbury, Harold
Police Commissioner who replaced **John McKinna**. Recommended to Premier **Don Dunstan** the appointment of New Scotland Yard detectives to investigate the Duncan case

SA Police Association
Police union

Seaman, the Rev. Keith
Methodist clergyman and future South Australian Governor; supported **gay law reform**

Smedley, Darryl
Uniformed constable who allegedly was warded off by **Francis Cawley** on the night of **Dr Duncan**'s death

Glossary

Spartacus
International gay travel guide carried by **Dr Duncan**

Stevenson, Derrance
Lawyer who represented **Mr X** at the inquest; killed in 1979 in the infamous 'Body in the Freezer' case

Sumner, Chris
Labor Attorney-General who announced a special task force following **Mick O'Shea**'s claims; tabled the **'Duncan Task Force Final Report'** in parliament

Tonkin, Dr David
Progressive **Liberal and Country League** member who introduced the 1972 **decriminalisation** Bill into the **House of Assembly**; also supported the 1975 Bill

Turner, Inspector Paul
Together with **Inspector Colin Lehmann** carried out the early police investigation of the Duncan case

University of Adelaide
Employed **Dr Duncan** through its Law School. Appointed **Bruce Debelle** to represent its interests and protect Duncan's reputation during the inquest

University of Adelaide footbridge
Footbridge which connects Victoria Drive with War Memorial Drive; together with **City Bridge** formed part of the **No. 1 Beat**

Vice Squad
Unit within SA Police whose members' duties included monitoring homosexual beats for criminal behaviour

The Death of Dr Duncan

von Einem, Bevan Spencer
Transported **Roger James** to hospital; convicted in 1984 of the murder of teenager Richard Kelvin

Williamson, Kevin
Gave evidence at the inquest of being warned away by two men – whom he later identified as **Michael Clayton** and **Brian Hudson** – from a spot where he could have witnessed the drowning

Witness A
see **Mr X**

Witnesses B, C and D
Gave evidence at the inquest of seeing groups of men fighting among the boatsheds on the night of **Dr Duncan**'s death. Their names are still protected

Image Acknowledgements

Adelaide Festival Front cover, 206 bottom

Cowan, Malcolm 109

Gay and Lesbian Counselling Service of SA Library 138

Glover, Alan 22

Hilliard OAM, Dr David 156

Markwell, Professor Kevin 32

National Archives of Australia 30

National Library of Australia viii

News Ltd/Newspix 36–37, 62, 75, 77, 79, 104, 122, 149, 151–52, 190–204

Purcell AM, Ian (renderer) iii, 189

Reeves, Tim 13, 43, 71, 86, 205, 206 top

Sergeant, Will Back cover

South Australian Coroner's Court 44, 98

South Australian Parliament Research Library 153, 177

State Records of South Australia 41

University of Adelaide 4, 29

Acknowledgements

This book had its genesis at Feast Festival under the direction of Helen Sheldon when the idea was first conceived for an event to mark the 50th anniversary of Dr Duncan's death. I applaud Helen's drive and vision. With the help of seed funding from Arts SA, the concept was developed to the point where Feast Festival, the Adelaide Festival and State Opera South Australia jointly commissioned the oratorio, *Watershed: The Death of Dr Duncan*, to be performed as part of the Adelaide Festival's 2022 program.

It was an honour to be appointed historical consultant for *Watershed* and to work with an extremely talented creative, production and management team. I especially acknowledge: Christie Anderson; Neil Armfield AO; Sean Bacon; Ruth Blythman; Steph Bone; Elaine Chia; Rachel Healy; Kate Hillgrove; Alan John; Nigel Levings; Lewis Major; Stuart Maunder; Lesley Newton; Ailsa Paterson; Cheryl Pickering; Jane Rosetto; Christos Tsiolkas; Dr Joe Twist; Zac Tyler; and Alana Valentine.

My publisher, Michael Bollen of Wakefield Press, responded quickly when I first pitched the book to him. I am also

Acknowledgements

grateful to Jo Dyer, Director of Adelaide Writers' Week, for the opportunity to participate in the 2022 event, and to Neil Armfield AO for helping to facilitate it.

I thank Will Sergeant who cheerfully spent many hours with me as we discussed and dissected the ins and outs of the Duncan case. I also thank Dr David Hilliard OAM who has always been a source of sage advice.

I record my appreciation of the staff of: Adelaide City Council; Department of the Premier and Cabinet; National Archives of Australia; National Library of Australia; South Australian Coroner's Court; South Australian Parliament; South Australian Parliament Research Library; State Library of South Australia; State Records of South Australia; and University of Adelaide.

I am greatly indebted to the following individuals, without whose assistance this book would not have been possible: William Makepeace Arnold; Andrew Cook; The Hon. Bruce Debelle AO, QC; Paul Foss; Dr Dino Hodge; Dr Paul Horrocks; James Johnston; Sara King; Marie Larsen; Stephen Leahy; Greg Mackie OAM; Fr Robert Mackley; Ian Maidment; Professor Kevin Markwell; Emeritus Professor Jill Julius Matthews; Tanya McPhedran; Kenton Penley Miller; Diane Myers; Paul Paech; Simon Royal; Jon Ruwolt; Michael Ryan; Mike Sexton; Robert Sims MLC; Patrick Stewart; Dr Nikki Sullivan; and Professor John Williams.

Index

Pages in bold refer to an illustration

A

Abbott QC, Michael 132–34, 211
ABC 2, 45, 52, 57, 76, 139, 154, 183
Abortion law reform 12
Adelaide Club 10
Adelaide Festival 3, 10, 188, 210, 224
Adelaide Law School 187
Advertiser 11, 35, **36–37**, 45, 48, 54, 58, **62**, 63, 71–73, **75**, 76–78, **79**, 80, 99, 101, 108, 112, 119, 121, 125, 127–28, 130–33, 143, 147–48, **149**, 150, **151–52**, 160, 162, 167, 171–73, 176, 179, 183, **199**, 207, 211
Agent-General 102
Ambassador's Hotel 31–**32**
American Psychiatric Association 175
Anal sex 80–81, 143
Anglicanism – *see* Religion
Anglo-Catholicism – *see* Duncan, Dr George Ian Ogilvie (Ian)
Atkinson, Michael 110–12, 211
Australian Democrats 130, 187
Australian Dictionary of Biography 1
Australian Psychological Society 175, 180
Australian Union of Students 45

B

Ball, Robert 130
Beat, No. 1 **13**, 31, **36–37**, 39, 46–47, 49, 53, 87, 119, 219
Beats 13–14, 31, 45, 47, 53, 58, 137, 144, 158
Beaumont case 77
Bennetts, Bill 157
'Body in the freezer' case – *see* Stevenson, Derrance
Boiled Sweets 167
Bray, John 9
Buckingham Arms Hotel 31–**32**, 50–51
Buggery – *see* Anal sex
Bulletin 175
Burdett, John 181

C

Callaghan, Robert (Bobby) 50–52, 133, 211
Cambridge 39
Cambridge University Press 28
CAMP – *see* Campaign Against Moral Persecution (CAMP) National/NSW/SA
Campaign Against Moral

Index

Persecution (CAMP) National 121
Campaign Against Moral
  Persecution (CAMP) NSW 146
Campaign Against Moral
  Persecution (CAMP) SA 72, 78,
  110, 146–47, 150, 154–55, **156**,
  157–59, 161–68, 171–72, 174–75,
  182, 211
CAMP INK **156**
Canary 166
Caribou Bar – *see* Buckingham
  Arms Hotel
Casey, Tom 161, 171–72, 182, 211
Castles, Professor Alex 39, 212
Catholicism – *see* Religion
Cawley, Francis 52, 63–68, 70, 84,
  87–92, 96–97, 99, 101–02, 112–19,
  121, 123, 130–31, 134–36, 191, **197**,
  200–01, 203–04, 212
Centennial Park Cemetery 70
Chamberlain case 132, 134
Channel 7 38
CHARLES – *see* Committee for
  Homosexual Law Reform in
  South Australia
Chatterton, Brian 173
Chief Secretary 72, 162
City Bridge 12–**13**, 31, 35, 83, 85, 88,
  90, 115–16, 212
City Coroner – *see* Cleland, Tom/
  Coroner/Coroner's inquest
Clayton, Michael 64, 66–70, 83,
  89, 91–92, 96–97, 99, 102, 112–18,
  121, 123, 130–32, 134–36, 191, **197**,
  200–01, 203–04, 212

Cleland, Tom 76, **77**, 78, 89, 93,
  100, **198**, 212 – also *see* Coroner/
  Coroner's Inquest/ Matheson,
  Rod
Cockburn, Stewart 124
Committee for Homosexual
  Law Reform in South Australia
  (CHARLES) 169, 212
Community Standards
  Organisation (CSO) – *see* Religion
Congregationalism – *see* Religion
Coroner 2–3, 77, 102, 108, 122, 190 –
  also *see* Cleland, Tom/Coroner's
  inquest/South Australian
  Coroner's Court
Coroner's inquest 38, 40, 42–**44**,
  47–52, 54–58, 69, 72, 76, Ch. 5, **79**,
  98, 101, 106, 108, 112–15, 121–23,
  125–26, 132–33, 143, 148, 150,
  190–98
Cottages 31
Court, Dr John 167, 174, 180, 182,
  212
Cowan, Malcolm 1
Creedon, Cec 173, 213
Crime and Punishment 140
Crime Stoppers SA 139
Criminal Investigation Bureau –
  see SA Police
Crown Solicitor 5, 78, 107–08

D

Debelle, Bruce 56, 78, 92, **190**, 213
Decriminalisation Bill, Britain 33,
  145

Decriminalisation Bill, South Australia
  1965 145
  1972 Ch. 8, **151–53**, 213
  1973 165–74
  1975 174–84, **177**
DeGaris, Ren 161, 164, 213
Draper, Laurence 107, **196**, **198**, 213
Dr Duncan Memorial Scholarship 187
Dr Duncan Revolution Bookshop 175
Dumas, Sir Lloyd 11
Duncan case **189–206**
  Abuse of Process 55, 134
  commemoration 1, 121, 185, 188
  'Duncan Task Force Final Report' 136–39, **138**, 214
  fourth man 93, 114, 123, 125–28, 132–33
  immunity from prosecution 79, 111, 129 – also see Mr X/ Witnesses B, C and D
  inquest – see Coroner's inquest
  New Scotland Yard report – see New Scotland Yard report
  pardon 102
  police cover-up 67, 76, 106, 120, 128, 133
  police investigation Ch. 4, **62**
  political cover-up 130–31
  preliminary hearing 47, 52, 59, 131–32, 135, **201–02**, 219
  reopening of Ch. 7, **200**
  reward 99, 129, 139

royal commission 71, 110, 129–30
trial Ch. 7, **203**
Duncan, Dr George Ian Ogilvie (Ian) **iii**, **43**, **189**, **198**, **200**, **202**, **204**, **206**, 213
  Adelaide, arrival in 29–31, **30**
  Anglo-Catholicism 16
  autopsy 39–**41**
  birth 15
  body, anal characteristics 80
  body, recovery of 35, 38
  Britain, life in 21–28
  burial 70
  childhood 17–19
  death 41–**43**, 121–22, **122**
  education (school) **viii**–ix, 17–18
  education (university) 18, 22–23, 28
  employment – see University of Adelaide/University of Bristol
  family – see Duncan, Hazel Kerr/ Duncan, Mary Magdalene (Billie)/Duncan, Ronald Ogilvie
  friendships 26–27
  High Court of Delegates, The 23, 34
  homosexuality 23–25, 27, 31–33, **32**, 93, 99
  Ian, known as 15
  inheritance 20–21
  interpretive sign 187, **206**
  martyrdom 188
  memorial plaque 187, **205**

Index

orphanhood ix, 20
personal effects 3, 38–39
personality 25–26, 33–34
physical description 35
Pride Walk 187, **205**
suitcase 1–2, 17, 20, 22, 26, 33, 213
tombstone 70–**71**
tuberculosis ix, 18–19, 21, 28
will 20–21
Duncan, Hazel Kerr 16–18
Duncan, Mabel 16
Duncan, Mary Magdalene (Billie) 16, 18, 20–21
Duncan, Peter 169–72, 174, 176–77, 183–84, 187, 213
Duncan, Ronald Ogilvie 15–18, 20, 33
'Duncan Task Force Final Report' – *see* Duncan case
Dunstan, Don 10–11, 49, 79, 91, 101–02, 108, 110, 124, 128, 139–40, 145–46, 154–55, 162–63, 169, 175, 183, 187, 214

E
Eastick, Dr Bruce 155, 214
Elections, South Australia
　1973 164–65, 168
　1975 174–75
　1985 129–30
Empire Times 46, 56

F
Female homosexuality 144
Ferrie, Margaret 161
Festival of Light – *see* Religion
Fitzgerald, Mr 116–17
Footbridge – *see* University of Adelaide footbridge
Foss, Paul 81, 110, 123–24, 214
Foster, Norm 181
Freedom of Information Act 110

G
Gay Activists Alliance (GAA) 166–69, 171–75, 181, 214
Gay law reform 214
　Australian Capital Territory 183
　New South Wales 183
　Northern Territory 183
　Queensland 183
　South Australia Ch. 8, Ch. 9
　Tasmania 183, 187
　Victoria 183
　Western Australia 183
Gay/Lesbian community/lobby groups – *see* Campaign Against Moral Persecution (CAMP) National/NSW/SA, Committee for Homosexual Law Reform in South Australia, Gay Activists Alliance, Gay Liberation, 'Radicalesbians'
Gay Liberation 166–67, 175, 215
Gay Pride Week 170
Gaytime Friendship Society, The 31
Geddes, Richard 172
Gielgud, John 145
Gilfillan, Gordon 172
Gill, B.N. viii–**ix**

Glover, Dorothy **22**–25, 27, 215
Glover, Harold 19–22, 27
Gresswell Tuberculosis Sanatorium 19

H
Hall, Steele 167
Harris, Ronald 88–89, 101, 116–17, **194**, 215
Henry VIII 23, 143
Hill, Murray **152**, 154–55, 157–59, 162–63, 168, 178, 186, 215
Hill, Robert 155
Hilliard, David 150
Hindmarsh, Phyllis 18–19, 24
Hiskey, Garry 55, 78, 215
Historical Journal 34
Holiday Inn 121–**22**
Homosexuality – *see* Female homosexuality/Male Homosexuality
Homosexuality in South Australia 165
Hopgood, Don 183
House of Assembly 11, 108, 155, 159, 162–64, 168, 170, 172, 178, 183, 215
Howell, Peter 34
Howie, Constable 118
Hudson, Brian 67–69, 83–84, 90–92, 97, 99, 102, 112–15, 117–18, 121, 123, 128, 130–32, 134, 136, 191, **197**, **200**–**02**, **204**, 215
Hudson, Hugh 172
Humanist Society of South Australia 148

I
Inquest – *see* Coroner's inquest
Internal Investigation Branch – *see* SA Police

J
James, Roger 35, 40–59, **43**–**44**, 67–75, 78, 80–82, 84–85, 86–88, 90, 92, 95–99, 105–06, 111–14, 118–19, 122–23, 128, 133–34, **192**, 215
Jonats, Mary 161
Joyce, Anne E. 160

K
Kadina Court of Summary Jurisdiction 130
Kanck, Sandra 187
Kelvin, Richard 42
Keogh, Henry 81
King, Len 74–76, **75**, 102, 108, 110, 160, 163, 215
King's Head Hotel 64, 69, 89–90, 123
King William Road/Street 12–13, 39, 46, 64, 69, 88, 94
Kintore Avenue 35, 54, 87, 93, 95–97
Knight, Roger 161, 174

L
Labor Party 10–12, 130, 145, 154–55, 161–64, 168–69, 173–76, 178, 182, 187, 216
Layton, Robyn 83, 216
Legislative Council/lor 155, 161, 164–65, 168, 171–72, 174–76, 178–79, 216

Index

Lehmann, Colin 64, 69, 74–75, 84, 89–91, 96, 108, 115, 128, **196, 198**, 216
Lenton, Noel 91, **75**, 216
Levy, Anne 180, 187, 216
Liberal and Country League Party (LCL) 9, 154–55, 159, 165, 168, 174, 216
Liberal Movement (LM) 11, 173, 176, 178, 216
Liberal Party 11, 129, 181, 216
Lincoln College 29, 39, 217
London Metropolitan Police 102
Lücke, Professor Horst 28–29, 31, 33, 70, 72–73, **75**, 80, 99, 217

M

Magistrates Courts
   Adelaide 57, 130–31
   Para Districts 130
   Perth 131
Major Crime Investigation Branch – *see* SA Police
Male homosexuality
   Adelaide sub-culture **32–33**, 71, 78, 144, 150 – also *see* Gay/Lesbian community/lobby groups
   agents provocateurs/decoys/entrapment 14, 53, 56, 58, 70, 79, 84, 119, 163, 185
   beats – also *see* Beat, No. 1/Beats
   British law 33
   criminalisation of 13–14, 47, 144, 147, 178
   discrimination against 147, 165, 167, 169, 175
   education about 172–73, 183–84
   English law 143
   marriage 160, 179
   media treatment of 78–**79**, 148–50, **149**, 150–**51**, 171–72, 176
   paedophilia 160
   parliamentary treatment of – *see* Decriminalisation Bill Britain/South Australia
   pathological treatment of 72, 80–82, 99
   police treatment of 14, 53, 65–66, 70, 74, 77, 91, 102, 110, 117–19, 126, 128, 136–39, 185 – also *see* SA Police: Vice Squad
   psychiatric treatment of 175, 178
   psychological treatment of 146, 175, 180, 187
   SA law 143–44
   sexual activity 81, 154, 160, 162
   State treatment of 14, 144, 148
   young bashers' treatment of 14, 53, 70, 74, 76
Manock, Dr Colin 39–40, 50, 80–81, 217
Manos, Nick 132, 134, 217
Martell – *see* Duncan, Hazel Kerr
Matheson, Rod 78, 82, 87, 89–90, 99, 108, **190**, 217
'Matter of Social Concern, A' 179–80
Maynard, Martin 88, 116, **195**, 217

McEwen, Mike 125, 128
McEwin, Sir Lyell 173, 176, 217
McGowan, Robert **104**, 104–07, 113, 115, **199**, 217
McKinna, John 63–64, 71–72, 77, 101–02, 217
McRae, Bob 89, **191**, 218
Melbourne Grammar School ix, 17
Melburnian **viii**–ix
Methodism – *see* Religion
Mildenhall, Edwin 64, 115, 124–25, 127–28, 218
Miles, John 148–50, **149**
Millhouse, Robin 110, 159, 178, 218
Mitchell Committee 147, 218
Mitchell, Justice Roma 146
Moles, Dr Robert 81
Monopoli, Tony 47, 99
Montagu of Beaulieu, Lord 145
Moral Action Committee (MAC) – *see* Religion
Moral Freedom Committee (MFC) 157, 218
Moral Re-Armament (MRA) – *see* Religion
Mr P 45, 55, 57, 124
Mr X 84–87, **86**, 94, 114, 118–19, **191**, 218
Mummie G 22
Murdoch, Rupert 11

N

National U 45, 49, 55, 57, 123–24
Nation Review 183

News 11, 58, 76, 99, **122**, 172, **198**, **200**, **202**
New Scotland Yard
  detectives 3, 47, 49, 52, 54, 83, 103–**104**, 106–08, 114, 119 – also *see* McGowan, Robert/O'Hanlon, Charles
  plaque 3–**4**, 219
  report 45, 49, 51, 57, Ch. 6, **109**, 125, 128, **199**, **204**, 219
New South Wales Council for Civil Liberties 183

O

O'Hanlon, Charles **104**, 104–07, **199**, 219
O'Loughlin, Maurice 135, 219
Orcades, SS 29
Osborne, Robert 87–88, 114–15, 219
O'Shea, Michael (Mick) 67, 92–93, 106, 118, 121–29, 131–36, 139, 185, **195**, **200**, 219

P

Parliament House 167
Perry, Bob 38
Playford, Tom 9–12
Police – *see* SA Police
Presbyterianism – *see* Religion
Private member's bill 11, 154, 164, 220 – also *see* Decriminalisation Bill, South Australia
Public Trustee 70

R

'Radicalesbians' 175

Index

Rayner, the Most Rev. Dr Keith 178–79, 220
Religion
  Anglicanism 16, **22**, 70, 147, 157, 165, 178, 180, 182
  Anglo-Catholicism – *see* Duncan, Dr George Ian Ogilvie (Ian)
  Catholicism 16, 147, 160, 180
  Community Standards Organisation 180, 212
  Congregationalism 147, 180
  Festival of Light 167, 174, 176, 180–81, 214
  Methodism 29, 147, 157, 180
  Moral Action Committee 12, 218
  Moral Re-Armament 157, 218
  Presbyterianism 16
Review 53, 71, 220
Rice, Paul 130–34, 220
Richards, Mrs 26
Rotoract 168
Royal Adelaide Hospital 35, 48, 123
Royal, Simon 2–3
Ruwolt, Jon 165–66, 169, 172, 175, 220

S

Salisbury, Harold 72, 91, 102–03, 107–08, **196**, **198–99**, 220
SA Police
  Criminal Investigation Bureau 64, 91, 127
  Internal Investigation Branch 136
  Major Crime Investigation Branch 2
  Underwater Recovery Squad 35
  Vice Squad x, 4–5, 14, 49, 53, 63–65, 67–68, 79, 84, 89, 93, 117, 119, 122–23, 125–28, 130, 134, 136–37, 163, 186, **197**, **201**, **203**, 221
SA Police Association 135–36, 220
Seaman, the Rev. Keith 157, 180, 220
Sigley, Ernie 167
Smedley, Darryl 88, 116, **195**, 220
Social Concern Committee 179–81
South Australian Coroner's Court 1
South Australian Council for Civil Liberties 170, 180
South Australian Parliament 12
South Park Lands 86
Spartacus 31–**32**, 50, 221
State Library of South Australia 2
State Public Service 165
State Records of South Australia 3
Stevenson, Derrance 84, 87, **191**, 221
St George's, Goodwood 16
Story, Ross 171
Sumner, Chris 129, 131, 136, 182, 221
Sunday Mail 76–77, 104, 155

T

Tardieu, Auguste-Ambroise 81
Tea rooms 31
This Day Tonight 38

Toledo Room – *see* Ambassador's Hotel
Tonkin, Dr David 159, 163, 178, 221
Torrens Beat – *see* Beat, No. 1
Torrens Lake – *see* Torrens, River/Lake
Torrens Parade Ground 82, 88, 95
Torrens Police Station 13, 64, 88, 101
Torrens, River/Lake x, 12, **13**, 14, 35, **36–37**, 40–41, 43, 45–48, 50, 65, 69, 74, 76, 82, 90, 93, 97, 105, 113, 115–18, 124, 126, 128, 158, 186, 188
Turing, Alan 145
Turner, Paul 64, 66, 74, 89, 91–92, 96, 108, 115, 127–28, 221

U

Underwater Recovery Squad – *see* SA Police
Universities
    Australian National 27
    Cambridge x, 22, 27–28, 31, 34
    Flinders 34, 46
    La Trobe 27
    Melbourne 27
    Monash 27
    of Adelaide 1, 12, 16, 26–27, **29**, 31, 39, 56, 78, 97, 221
    of Bristol x, 25–28, 31
    of Cardiff 27
    of Edinburgh 27
    of Exeter 27
    of Leicester 27
    of Oxford 27

University of Adelaide footbridge 12–**13**, 31, 35, 46, 121, 187, 221

V

Vice-Chancellor 33, 73
Vice Squad – *see* SA Police
Victimless crime 169
Victoria Drive 12, 31, 39, 42, 46, 54, 57, 64, 82–84, 86, 88, 90, 93, 95–96, 115
Victoria Park Racecourse 121
von Einem, Bevan Spencer 42, 56–58, **193**, 222

W

Walkley Award 125
Ward, Peter 169
Watershed: The Death of Dr Duncan 3, 188, **206**, 224
West Terrace Mortuary 39
Who's Who in Gay & Lesbian History 81
Williamson, Kevin 51, 68, 82–83, 94–95, 97, 114, 117–19, **194**, 222
Witness A – *see* Mr X
Witnesses B, C and D 49, 51–52, 83–84, 92–93, 106, 111, 114, 117, 122, 133, 222
Wolfenden Report 145

Z

'Zapping' 167

Wakefield Press is an independent publishing and
distribution company based in Adelaide, South Australia.
We love good stories and publish beautiful books.
To see our full range of books, please visit our website at
www.wakefieldpress.com.au
where all titles are available for purchase.
To keep up with our latest releases, news and events,
subscribe to our monthly newsletter.

Find us!

Facebook: www.facebook.com/wakefield.press
Twitter: www.twitter.com/wakefieldpress
Instagram: www.instagram.com/wakefieldpress

www.ingramcontent.com/pod-product-compliance
Lightning Source LLC
Chambersburg PA
CBHW051054230426
43667CB00013B/2296